So You're A Teenage Girl

Distributed by

CHOICE BOOKS

Salunga, Pa. 17538

We welcome your response

So You're A Teenage Girl

Jill Renich

Zondervan Publishing House
Grand Rapids, Michigan

SO YOU'RE A TEENAGE GIRL
Copyright 1966 by Zondervan Publishing House
Grand Rapids, Michigan

Zondervan Publishing House
1415 Lake Drive, S.E.
Grand Rapids, Michigan 49506

Library of Congress Catalog Card Number 66-13690
ISBN 0-310-31802-5

Printed in the United States of America

84 85 86 87 88 89 90 / 40 39 38 37 36 35 34 33

*To my three lively girls who demonstrate
the fun of being a teen:*

JANET

ROSALIE

JACQUELINE

Preface for TEENS

"Oh, Mother," bubbled my eldest daughter, "Don't you wish you were a teenager!!?"

"No, I *don't,* honey. But I love being the mother of one who is enjoying life so much!"

My teen years were spent away from home in missionary boarding schools (about which I could write volumes), and they were years of struggle. As I sought help from the books I read, either the girls were beautiful and perfect, or ugly and hopeless. I would love to have read a book about ordinary girls who were sometimes good, sometimes bad, girls who were trying and growing.

Through the months I have been writing, the girls in my book have become my friends as they have been living, learning, loving, and growing in Christian character. None of them is perfect, none hopeless. Now I want to share them with you. Their experiences are similar to those of my own daughters and their many friends.

My warmest thanks go to Jean Sudyk whose daily prayers and persistent help encouraged me. To Peggy Thompson who faithfully typed the manuscript. To the teens who read it and contributed their ideas. To the many friends who prayed. To my own precious children for their willing extra help around the house. To Nancy who came faithfully every day. And most of all to the wonderful father of our own teenagers who prayed and prodded me on.

JILL RENICH

Detroit, Michigan

CONTENTS

So You're A Teenage Girl

1

Dreams for Tomorrow

"That teacher!" Jan tossed and turned in her comfortable bed. "What does *she* know about being a teenager?"

Banging her pillow into a more comfortable lump, Jan thought about the provoking remark Miss Marshall made to her during lab class.

"Be tomorrow or next year what I am today? Yuk, it makes me sick," she thought as she pulled the blanket under her chin. Jan mumbled to herself, "So you're a teenage girl!" Flipping over onto her stomach and hugging her pillow, she thought more calmly, "What I am today is what I'll be tomorrow, and the day after, and the day after. But I'd sure hate to go on like this forever. What a day! From the minute I came home everything went wrong."

"Jan, you left your room in a mess this morning," Mother accused. "Make your bed right away, then come down and set the table . . . ."

That did it.

"Make your bed; set the table; put the kids to bed; do your homework . . . . What a life!"

"Do you realize, Jan, that we can tell pretty well what you will be like when you grow up, by what you are like now?" Miss Marshall's remark re-echoed.

"Oh, dear! I don't want to be like this when I grow up!"

"What do I want to be like?" Jan thought. "I'd hate to be like Miss Burns who is so dull and crabby. I'd love to be like Mrs. James, always smiling and happy. She's never in a hurry, and has time to talk to all of the kids . . . and she's so sweet to her children . . . . There is such love in her home, and —

"I wonder what Mrs. James was like when she was a teenager? I wonder if she had problems . . . ."

Jan thought of her own shortcomings: her moodiness, her attitude toward the younger children, how angry she became with her mother. She thought of the times when she felt she couldn't stand to look at Barbara, her rival at school, and she realized this was not the kind of person she wanted to be all the rest of her life.

"I wonder," she thought grimly, "if this was the way Miss Burns was at my age."

Troublesome thoughts. She would have a talk with Mrs. James as soon as she could, perhaps Sunday.

After church on Sunday Jan looked around for Mrs. James. "Oh, I do hope she is here," she thought. "She never misses unless one of the children is sick, but it would just be my luck to have her home today when I want to talk to her so badly."

After church Jan glanced back to the row where Mrs. James usually sat. Yes, there she was, looking so young and attractive. She was smiling at her rambunctious five-year-old as she helped him to put on his coat.

Jan tried not to be too obviously pushing her way

through the crowded aisle, but *why* were there so *many* people at church today! By the time she reached the back of the church, Mrs. James was shaking hands with the minister at the door.

"How I did appreciate your message today," Jan heard her say warmly. "It helped me to see my need for more love and patience, and the answer that God has for me."

"Oh," thought Jan, "does *she* have problems? I can't imagine her with any problems, but then maybe that is why she can understand us so well, and why the kids like to talk to her."

At the foot of the steps Jan touched Mrs. James's arm. As she turned to see who touched her, the warmth of her manner made Jan feel better immediately.

"Hi, Jan, where have you been lately? I haven't seen you in quite a while — at least to talk to."

"Exams have kept me busy. But say, Mrs. James, could I come over to see you this afternoon or some afternoon after school next week?"

"I'd love to have you, Jan." Mrs. James was obviously pleased. "But this afternoon we are having some out-of-town guests. Could you come over Tuesday, after school?"

The thought of having to wait three days was hard for Jan to accept. "Yes," she thought, "that is part of my trouble too. I want what I want when I want it — no patience!" But she hid her impatience, saying, "I'll really be looking forward to coming."

At 6:30 the alarm rang. Jan shut it off sleepily. "If I skip my Bible reading this morning I can sleep

15 minutes more . . . ." "But you need your time with God to start the day right," said the faint voice of conscience. "Yes, but I got to bed too late last night and with an extra fifteen minutes I'll be able to work better in school today."

Jan reset the alarm.

At 6:45 it rang again, right in the middle of a luscious dream. Groggily she staggered out of bed to dress. "What'll I wear?" she thought, dimly wishing she'd decided the night before. But she couldn't because Mother was cross with her for washing her hair so late, and she hardly let her set it, much less pick out her clothes for school the next day.

"Mmmmm, the pink skirt won't do. I wore that yesterday. Can't wear the black one, all the kids are sick of it."

"Jan," called Mother, not too patiently. "Hurry, or you'll miss the bus — and remember, you *must* eat breakfast."

"If only Mother would leave me alone, I'd make out just fine, but she's always checking on me," thought Jan resentfully.

"Jan," came Mother's voice again, and this time a little more sharply. "Jan, did you hear what I said? Answer me!"

"Yes, I heard you. Of course, I *always* eat breakfast."

"What about last Friday?" reminded Mother, not too sweetly.

"But I'd have been late for the bus, Mother. You know that."

"That's just what I mean," said Mother. "Now hurry. You only have five minutes."

"The utter utter unreasonableness of mothers" Jan thought to herself, and if she had dared, she'd have a few other things to say to this mother of hers, but she let the matter drop. Grabbing the tweed dress, she threw it on over her head. If Mother hadn't wasted her time talking to her, she'd be dressed by now! "Oh, rats, where's the belt?"

"Jan —" from the doorway.

"Mother, I can't find my belt. Yes, I know, if I'd put it where it belongs . . . ."

At last, breakfast.

"Jan, sit down while you eat. Don't just stand there at the sink gulping your breakfast."

"Mother, can't you see I'm nearly late now? I haven't time to sit down to eat."

"Then you'll have to get to bed earlier so that you can get up earlier and have time for the things you need to do."

"Oh, Muh-thur —"   "I bet Lucy doesn't have all this trouble with her mother," thought Jan as she bolted the last mouthful of food, grabbed her school books, lunch and coat, and ran for the bus.

"Bye, Mother, see you after school. Oh, no — not tonight, I have glee club practice."

On the bus there was little time to think. "Oh, Jan, what a darling hair style," commented Lucy.

"It really shines in the light," added Karin.

"Anyway," thought Jan, "even tho' Mother is always crabbing at me, the girls like me as I am." With that the world and its troubles began to fade as the girls chatted happily on their way to school.

Jan could hardly wait for fourth hour — Lit. Miss Gay was lovely, so young and full of life. What a difference a teacher can make to a class. Miss Gay's name suited her perfectly; she always seemed so happy.

But Jan felt a little uneasy. She had just dashed off the paper she'd handed in on Friday. "But I couldn't help that," thought Jan defensively. "The Whirling Teens," her favorite TV program was on Thursday night. "After all, I don't waste a lot of time on TV. There are not that many programs I like, and I do need *some* time for fun."

Miss Gay came into the room as the bell rang. She really looked sharp in her new red suit. Smiling, she greeted the class. "Some teachers make you really *want* to study," thought Jan. "And others . . . ." Her thoughts were arrested as Miss Gay began to speak.

"Class, you remember I told you at the beginning of the year that the editor of the *Daily Times* was looking for a junior editor and that he has always picked one from this class after the year has begun. Today is the day. Mr. Owens will select his editor from the papers you handed in Friday."

Jan's heart sank. Of all the activities, she wanted most to be the junior editor. Other young people were good at athletics, but she wasn't, so in that area she didn't have a chance. However in writing she could compete. Why hadn't Miss Gay told them they would be judged on *this* paper. It wasn't fair. She'd have skipped the TV program if she had known.

"I'm sorry I couldn't warn you all ahead, but you see I didn't know myself until Mr. Owens called me after school and asked if I had any papers from which he could select his junior editor. So today is an exciting day. After school Mr. Owens will call me and let me know his decision. I had a chance to glance over your papers before Mr. Owens came for them. Some looked good, and others looked like they had been done in a hurry and you didn't have time to copy them neatly. Those papers I hated to give to Mr. Owens. He might think I'm a sloppy teacher," she ended with her lovely laugh.

"Her — a sloppy teacher?" thought Jan aghast. "The beautifully groomed Miss Gay, sloppy? *She* couldn't help it if the students handed in sloppy work — or could she . . . ?"

The class period dragged. Jan felt worse and worse about her paper. With a little more time she really could have developed her theme. The idea was good.

Chemistry class was worse than usual. Her eyes kept straying to the clock. "How can any teacher be so boring, and what's the point in studying something so utterly useless and ridiculous. It has nothing — absolutely nothing — to do with present-day living."

Three o'clock at last. That bell somehow rang differently — an alive, vibrant, joyous, "it is finished" sort of ring. Oh, the relief at the end of a day, the happy brushing and jostling of kids through the halls, the bus ride home, boy talking to girl, girl giggling with girl.

"Hi, Mom, I'm home!"

"How was your day?" Mother asked from the stove.

"Oh, Mother, of all things. You know how much I hoped to be junior editor of the *Daily Times*."

"Yes?"

"Well, Miss Gay gave the papers we handed in Friday to Mr. Owens and he's going to select the junior editor from those. And Mother," groaned Jan,

"I had a real good idea, but I just didn't have time to develop it."

"How was that? Didn't the teacher give you enough time?"

"She told us a week ago, but Mother, she never said that Mr. Owens might want *those* papers. She should have reminded us."

"You're not in grade school anymore, you know" remarked her mother dryly.

"But Mother, I don't think it's fair. She could have warned us that she might use those."

"What's the matter? Did you hand in a sloppy paper?"

"Oh, Muh-thur, you're no help," and with that Jan slammed up to her room and threw everything on the bed.

"What's the use of trying? Nothing turns out right anyway. Mother doesn't understand. Miss Gay didn't play fair."

A small voice came from within, "Did you honestly do your best? Did Miss Gay *have* to tell you again Thursday, when she had mentioned it several times before? Why are you so angry because your mother mentioned a sloppy paper?"

"But it isn't fair that we have to be judged on that one paper."

"You're not a child anymore," came the small voice, "you're in high school and shouldn't have to be reminded again and again of the same thing."

"What a pain to grow up! Why can't I just be like Miss Gay or Mrs. James all-of-a-sudden-like?"

Her thoughts were jarred by her Mother's voice calling,

"Jan, would you set the table for me, please?"

"But I have homework, why can't Lyn do it?"

"She did it last night, and I think there's time to finish your homework after supper."

"Oh, all right," assented Jan in an unpleasant voice.

"I know you're upset Jan, but you don't have to take it out on the rest of the family."

"I'm not upset," snapped Jan.

"How about a smile," said Mother in her irritatingly "nice" voice.

It had been a long day. A test in chemistry tomorrow. What a bore to study for it. If only she could re-do her paper. At last it was bedtime. Better pray tonight, since there wasn't time this morning.

"Dear Lord, I'm sorry I didn't do my best on that paper, but, please Lord, give me another chance and somehow let Mr. Owens select me. And help me to be nice *all* the time. Amen."

2

A Shattered Dream Today

The chatter of the girls on their way to school could be heard above the noisy motor of the bus.

"I hope my paper is chosen. I'll just die if it isn't," moaned Jan. "I hope so too," agreed Lucy. "It should be chosen. After all, aren't you the best writer in the class?"

"I don't know about that, but I do know I handed in one of the worst papers I've done for a long time. I had a good idea, but . . . ," and her voice trailed off as the other girls began discussing the pros and cons of the latest haircuts the boys had. June switched the subject.

"My mother's sure old-fashioned. She thinks the way girls wear their hair today looks ridiculous."

"So does mine," echoed Terry.

"Mine doesn't care; she never says anything one way or the other," put in Karin.

"My mother and I were talking at breakfast this morning and she thinks the way I'm doing my hair now is real cute. She hadn't said much before, but she says she's glad I'm over the fad," said Jan. "Now that I think of it, it did look pretty silly."

"Do you mean you *talk* to your mother, Jan?" asked Karin. "I'd never tell my mother anything or ask her opinion either. She's so old-fashioned she doesn't know what's going on anyway."

"Oh, *I* would. Sometimes I get pretty mad at mine, but we have some good talks. She asks my opinion about a lot of things and takes my suggestions, and lots of times, after we have talked things over, I see she has some pretty good ideas."

"I wish I could talk to *my* mother," added Karin wistfully. "But lots of times she isn't home when I get there, and other times, when I try to talk to her she doesn't act very interested."

"Not mine," said Jan. "Sometimes I wish she weren't *quite* so interested, but I guess you can't have everything! Your mother is probably a lot more interested than she acts. You should try talking to her."

Fourth hour took forever rolling around today. Miss Gay seemed to look as pretty in the aqua dress today as she looked in the red suit yesterday. The color was so alive. Jan had never noticed the deep blue of her eyes. "My," thought Jan, "she ought to wear aqua all the time."

Miss Gay started right in on the subject uppermost in the thoughts of the class. "I had a talk with Mr. Owens today. He had some rather interesting things to say about your papers. In the first place, he felt that they were some of the best high school papers he had read. You don't know how good that made me feel since this is my first year here! In the last school where I taught they did not select a junior editor from the school for the local paper. Really, it's a wonderful idea. And what experience it is for the one who has the honor!"

Miss Gay could see that the young people were becoming more and more restless. "Please, don't become impatient," she added, "because before I tell you whom Mr. Owens chose, I want to share with you some of the comments he made about your papers.

"First, he thought Fred had a very clear style of writing. He knew what he wanted to say and could get right to the point.

"Mr. Owens felt Bill wrote with vigor and crispness.

"Jan's paper showed real originality and thought.

"But Barbara's paper, Mr. Owens felt, combined most of these characteristics. The paper contained few mistakes and looked like it had been worked and reworked for the best effect.

"Unfortunately some of the papers seemed to be

a little carelessly done." Jan could feel the blood rush to her face. Who else could he mean but her, but, oh, how thankful she was that Miss Gay was not naming any names now!

Heartsick, Jan left class that day. "And Barbara, of all people. Why did it have to be Barbara? Barbara always seems to get the breaks. It isn't fair trying to compete against her. After all, she is a lot smarter than I am," thought Jan.

One happy thought for the day however; this was the afternoon Mrs. James was free. It couldn't have come at a better time. Mrs. James would understand, or maybe she wouldn't. She may never have had troubles like this. Anyway it would be good to talk to her, Jan decided.

Mrs. James greeted Jan warmly with her usual smile of welcome. It was flattering to feel that Mrs. James really liked her. "Jan, it is so good to see you. It seems like a long time since you were in my Sunday school class and we used to have those good discussions. How are things going at school? Have any interesting teachers this year? Come on in. I was sure you'd be hungry after school so I fixed us a snack."

Jan was anticipating the talk, but the suggestion for something to eat sounded great. It would be much easier to talk while eating.

"Thank you so much, Mrs. James, for taking the time to have me over this afternoon. I hate to bother anyone with my troubles, but I thought you might be able to help me.

"School's okay, and I like my teachers, especially

my Lit teacher, Miss Gay. But today I feel pretty awful."

"Why, Jan?"

"Well, you see, we all handed in a Lit paper Friday and, of all things, Mr. Owens took them to choose his junior editor."

"What was wrong with that?"

"Everything was wrong with it. In the first place Miss Gay didn't warn us that we might be judged on that paper. I had a good idea, but didn't have time to work it over very well."

"Doesn't Miss Gay give you enough time to do your assignment?"

"It wasn't exactly that, Mrs. James. Well, you see, well — to be perfectly honest with you — I watched my favorite program on TV Thursday night. Then I kept on watching. Before I knew it my time was gone and I had to throw my paper together in order to get it done."

"How do you feel about that?"

"I feel mad. I'm mad at Miss Gay for not telling us and I'm mad at Barbara for winning. Barbara always gets the breaks."

"Always?"

"Well, almost always, but that's not the point."

"The point being that you are really mad at yourself?"

"Yes, I guess you're right. I really know I could do better and I want to do better, but I don't. What's wrong with me?"

"Could it be that you find it easier to do what you *want* to do rather than what you *ought* to do?"

"I guess you're right. It is much easier to look

at TV than to do homework, and the programs were good and one of them was real educational."

"But was it worth loosing the editorship of the paper for?"

"Not really, I suppose."

"You know, Jan, when I was younger I had the most awful time putting 'first things first.'"

"*You* did?"

Mrs. James laughed. "I wouldn't like to say I *did*, because I still struggle over this, but I am improving. I found it was a bad habit I was getting into, but it didn't bother me much until I was 'caught' one day. My mother had been warning me over and over that if I didn't stop putting things off and doing them at the last minute I'd be sorry some day.

"I was in the band at school and just loved every minute of it, but I hated sewing and ironing. One weekend the President was to pay a special visit to our town and *our* band was to play for his welcome. You can imagine the excitement. The day came and I was so excited I couldn't eat any breakfast. Mother warned me I'd probably feel faint as it was apt to be a long day. I threw on my uniform only to find it had a rip under the arm, down where it could be seen. I knew the rip was there, but had put off sewing it up. It was getting later and later, but I tore off the jacket and started to mend it. Putting it back on again I rushed downstairs, picked up my French horn and started for the door when Mother called me, "Louise, look at your skirt. It looks like you slept in it. Did you hang it on the floor last night?" I was furious. There was no time to press my skirt *now*. Mother persisted.

"Honey, you don't want to play for the President looking like that do you?" Of course I didn't, but what could I do. The other young people were catching the eight-ten, but it was eight now and it took me seven minutes to make it to the corner. What should I do!

"Take off your skirt, honey, and I'll press it for you," said Mother sweetly.

"Oh, Mother, what'll I do? Why didn't you tell me sooner?"

"I didn't *see* you sooner. Here, let me have it and I'll have it done in a minute." Mother whipped out the ironing board and really did it in a hurry without even an, "I told you so." I tore down the street, but as I rounded the corner to the stop I could see the last of the gang getting on the bus. The door closed and the bus rolled away. No one could hear my shouts.

"It was fifteen minutes before the next bus and fifteen minutes of agonized thoughts. Why hadn't I mended the rip when I first saw it? Why hadn't I checked the skirt and ironed it the night before? I felt sick to my empty stomach. The band director wouldn't tolerate lateness and I could hardly cover being fifteen minutes later than the rest. To make a long story short I was just behind all day long and all the fun went out of that exciting day.

"It taught me a lesson about putting things off. Mother was a doll and never mentioned it again."

"I know just how you felt," said Jan sympathetically.

"Not only that, Jan, but our Sunday school lesson the next day was on the five wise and the five foolish virgins.[1] The teacher really made it vivid about the

[1] Matthew 25:1-13

unpreparedness of the five foolish virgins and all that they missed and all that they could have had with just a little forethought. It put a wholesome fear into me. Someday there would be something really important, more important than the band concert and, because of my carelessness, I'd miss God's best for me."

"I see what you mean. I've always heard the story of the virgins, but I never thought of it as applying to me, but it sure does today. Last night I prayed I'd get the editorship, but that didn't work either."

"Do you think it would have been right to be rewarded for work that was not your best?"

"Yes, but I wasn't going to do it again. I learned my lesson."

"But had you really?"

"I — I guess you're right, Mrs. James, if I had gotten by this time I'd have probably tried the same thing again later."

"You know, Jan, the thing that God is really interested in is *Christian character*. He is developing 'Commandos of the Cross,' not 'chocolate soldiers' that melt in the sun. God knows our weaknesses. He wants us to see them so that we will come to Him and ask for His power and His strength to overcome them. If God hadn't begun to meet me in this area, I would never be able to share with you His power, but I *know* He can help, because He is helping me to do the *right* thing, not just the *easy* thing. But you must *ask* Him."

"I think I'm beginning to see what you mean. I've never forgotten the talk you gave in Sunday school about giving a day's work for a day's wage, but I'd never connected it with doing my best on my homework. After your talk, I sure changed on the way I was doing my baby-sitting jobs. Before, I'd just sit with the kids and if they needed to be entertained I'd do that, but I was always glad when they were in bed so I could have an evening of uninterrupted reading. Now, since I'm being paid, I look around to see what needs to be done; if I don't have too much homework, I do the dishes and try to tidy the house a bit.

"Thanks so much for the talk, Mrs. James. There's a lot of other things I'd like to talk to you about, but I've got to run. Mother will be looking for me, and I'd hate for her to be mad at me on top of the rest!"

"It's been fun talking to you, Jan. Being a teen-ager isn't the easiest thing in the world, but it certainly is challenging. Come back soon."

3

A Ruined Day

"Oh, Mother," Jan burst in the door from school. "Oh, Mother, that Barbara gives me a pain. Ever since she won the junior editorship she will hardly speak to me. She's just too busy. She's been real buddy — buddy with Lucy and Marti too. She makes me sick! She even asked Marti to do an article on our Chem class and there *I* was. The least she could have done would have been to ask me."

"You find her pretty hard to take, don't you, honey?"

"I sure do! She really thinks she's great. You should see the way she plays up to Fred and Bill. Wanting their help, my foot! She wants their attention. They don't even see through her and are helping her on her articles. Boy, if they can't see through that, they sure are blind."

"Did you offer to help her with her articles?"

"Me? I should say not. Not that snob. She asked for the job. I didn't."

"Honey! What a way to talk!"

"It's the truth. You ought to see how she shines up to Miss Gay and spends extra time with her. The rest of us can't get near her. Oh, Mother, I wish I could die. Everything is going wrong. What's the use of praying and the Bible is so boring. Anyway, what's the use of life . . . . I'm going to bed!"

"You don't sound like yourself. You must be tired. It's Lyn's turn to set the table. I'll call you for supper."

Supper was a rather gloomy affair. There seemed to be a cloud over everyone as Jan sat quietly and dejectedly ate her supper.

"What's the matter with Jan?" chirped her seven-year-old brother.

"Don't you feel good?" asked Lyn, sympathetically.

"No, I don't," snapped Jan.

"Wow, it sure doesn't sound like it," commented Rick.

Jan went to her room and tried to study. A few days ago life had been worth living, but now everything seemed to be going wrong. She labored through her subjects. "Good night," she called to her mother earlier than usual.

"I'll be up in a minute, honey."

"Good night," her dad called up to her.

"Honey," he said turning to his wife, "what is the matter with Jan? Something go wrong at school?"

"Yes and no. It is one of those situations where one thing leads to another until the world is tumbling about your head. She didn't do her best on a paper, so one of her friends got the junior editor's job, and now she is being eaten up with jealousy — though she can't see that's what it is."

"What are you going to do about it? We can't let this go on. It's affecting the whole family."

"I'm going up now to talk to her."

Jan felt the comfort of her mother's presence as she sat on the side of her bed. How sweet and understanding her mother looked in the semi-darkness of her bedroom.

"Honey, I know how awful you feel. I'll never forget the unhappy time I had in high school with one of my friends. She was my best friend, and we were in a poster contest. Of course we talked over our ideas. Then she took the best idea I had and insisted it was her own, so I had to think up something else. She won the contest."

"Oh, Mother, that's not fair!"

"But that wasn't all. I became so resentful I couldn't speak to her; though she did her best to make things right. I was filled with bitterness toward her and loved nursing it.

"I *was* awful to her. Of course we drifted apart as friends, but I didn't care. At least I never let on that I really did care. After a few weeks, we had a vacation and I went north to see my grandmother. She *would* have to ask me how it was I lost the poster contest. That was all I needed to pour out all my resentment against Ginny.

"Grandmother didn't mince any words with me. She went right to her worn old Bible and turned to Hebrews 12:15. She showed me the fearful consequences of allowing bitterness to dominate my heart. It was driving me away from God and opening my heart and life to the power of Satan. And worse than that — it was hurting others. Finally I saw what I had done to Ginny. I saw how jealous I had been and how I had turned one of her friends away from her. I was sick. Grandmother and I prayed together, and I told God how sorry I was for the way I had been acting and asked Him to forgive my sin — my selfishness and my jealousy of Ginny. I promised Him I'd make it right with her as soon as I got home."

"Did you?"

"Yes, I certainly did. God taught me a lesson I've never forgotten.

"Darling, your anger and hatred toward Barbara are really sins against God. He has commanded us to *love* one another, and what is more, Jesus taught that we are not to come to God to seek His forgiveness if we refuse to forgive others.

"Bitterness grows in our hearts when the first seed is allowed in. It affects everyone you contact. Remember dinner tonight? Remember how rude you were to Rick and Lyn? You'd be surprised at the gloom you spread in the whole house tonight,"

"I don't want to be selfish and hateful, but I don't want to love Barbara either."

"Are you willing to ask God's forgiveness?"

"Yes."

"Are you willing to ask Him to fill your heart with love for Barbara?"

There was a long pause as a multitude of thoughts raced through Jan's mind. It felt so good to hate Barbara; she deserved to be hated — but Jan didn't want to disobey God!

Suddenly the love of God toward her in spite of all her hatred, flooded over her. She realized how much He loved Barbara. By contrast she saw the wickedness of her hatred. Was she willing? How could she be otherwise? She *must* love Barbara. She would . . . .

"Yes, Mother."

"In the quiet atmosphere of deep understanding, mother and daughter knelt before God. Jan asked for forgiveness and love. A peace flooded her heart such as she had not had before. Love for God welled up inside her. The battle was over.

"Good night, darling."

"Thank you, Mother. Good night."

4

Snow Retreat

Between semesters — what a glorious time of year! Somehow it is even more exciting than summer vacation, for the days are few and precious. All the drag of the first semester can be forgotten, now that exams are over and a few carefree days are ahead.

Jan, the gang at church, and some of her school friends had planned to go to a winter camp for girls up north where the snow was deep and the ice was good. Winter sports were such fun, but some camp speakers were so dull that they nearly spoiled all the fun. Why were there so few interesting speakers for teenagers? Either you got someone who talked down to you or you got someone that acted silly trying to sound like a teenager.

The long bus ride to camp was full of fun and excitement. Once the battered old bus slid off the icy road. Another time a few stragglers failed to show up after a short lunch stop and were accidently left behind!

The bus was filled with the pent-up steam of a long semester. When the bus doors finally opened at the camp, the young people came scrambling out, yelling and screaming. Snowballs flew in all directions.

"Top bunk in the first dorm," Jan yelled as she picked up her things, staggering under their weight toward the dorm.

"A lower bunk for me," chimed in Lucy, grabbing her bags and following Jan.

The dorm felt warm in contrast to the crisp air outside.

"Hot cocoa is being served in the lodge," someone shouted from the doorway.

Sleeping bags were tossed on beds claimed by their owners, then there was a dash for the lodge. An enormous fire was burning in the fireplace at one end of the lodge. The girls gathered around it with cups of steaming cocoa and hot doughnuts.

"Come on over here and sit with me, Lucy," called Jan. "Say did you hear that we're going to have devotions after cocoa?"

"Oh," groaned Lucy in a low voice, "I hope they won't be too long — and *boring*," she added.

A few minutes later the buzz of chatter was interrupted by the Camp Director welcoming the group. She announced a devotional by one of the Camp Counselors.

A young woman with a friendly smile stood up and started right in.

"Some years ago in China the Japanese were taking over the country. Many of the Americans were interned during this time. However, the day came when some of the Americans were to be repatriated. The missionaries were busy packing the few possessions they were allowed to take with them. One Japanese guard approached a missionary and asked her what possession she prized most highly. Believing this to be kindness on the part of the soldier, she said, 'My stamp collection.' Then and there the missionary was relieved of her stamps. Had she not cared, the stamps would be hers today.

"Girls, the Bible tells us of a man who dealt in valuable pearls. He searched continually until he found the pearl of greatest value. When he found it he sold everything he owned to buy it. What do you value? If God gave you a choice of anything you wanted, what would *you* choose? What do you *really* want from life? What you want will determine the direction your life will take.

"If you value material things — like stamps — they will be taken from you when you leave this 'country.' If you value God's will most of all, then His riches will be yours forever.

"When you go to your cabins tonight, I want you to think. What is the most important thing in your life? Friends? Boys? Popularity? Success?

"Are you willing to count the cost and give yourself to God to seek that which He values for you?"

The talk ended with a short prayer.

"Boy, she really gave us something to think about," remarked Karin, "but I'm not so sure I want to give myself to God. I'd hate to have to read my Bible and pray all the time."

"Yeah, but she sure looks like she's enjoying life," observed Lucy.

"Why are you so quiet, Jan?" Karin asked.

"Now don't laugh, but I was *thinking*. How do values pertain to us in high school? How could we be any different? Our life is pretty much cut out for us — school and home. But what's the purpose of it all?"

"Let's ask her tomorrow," suggested Lucy, and with that the girls raced to the cabin to make up their bunks.

Who has more fun than a gang of girls — short-sheeting beds, tying knots in the arms and legs of pajamas, and chatting late into the night? But *who* has more trouble getting up in the morning?

The breakfast bell brought action to the sleepy girls who began throwing on their clothes with great haste. No one wanted to miss breakfast or the tobogganing afterward.

"I thought this camp would be boring with no boys around," remarked Karin, "but it is sort of fun not to be worrying about them!" The girls laughed — much to Karin's embarrassment — but they laughed because they had all been thinking the same thing.

The snow was perfect for tobogganing, but by mid-morning they were ready for a hot drink and some sweet rolls.

The warmth of the glowing fire made them all drowsy, but they came to when the topic of the morning talk was announced to be "Date Bait."

"A girl who is not popular with the boys feels like she has really missed something in her life," Mrs. MacDonald began. "She feels as though she has something seriously wrong with her. She may be plenty popular with the girls. But that's not much comfort when there is no boy hanging on to her every word, offering to take her home, and dating her to every important function in school. What is it that seems to make some girls so popular — so effortlessly too! Why do boys pass up some really lovely girls?

"It is fun to have lived long enough to watch boys growing up. Their reactions to girls change with their age. In the middle teens, boys seem to go for the cute girls. These girls attract boys, but the attraction is not necessarily based on the character of the girl. It is often based on sex appeal. Boys are drawn to them, but they really don't know why. Often, when this appeal is cultivated, it leads to an early teen marriage. But because there has not been time for character development, many marriages fail. There has been little solid basis for this important relationship.

"You girls who are not dating at this time should take the opportunity to develop in your character and personality an attractiveness that runs deeper than a surface appeal of good looks or sex. How can you do this? Let me give you a list of character traits that each of you should have to be a person well worth knowing:

> Self-control
> Even disposition
> Friendliness
> Dependability
> Consideration toward family
> Thoughtfulness toward others
> Cooperation in group projects
> Ambition
> Persistence
> Carefulness in appearance
> Keeping healthy
> Positive attitude toward life.

"I suggest you list these character traits in the back of your Bible, and check yourself from time to time. Watch the progress you are making.

"Boys in their later teens prefer another type of girl. Sex appeal may enter in, but they are looking more for character, though they might not know how to define it. These boys appreciate sincerity. They like girls who are interested in them. They like girls with whom they can talk freely. They appreciate being challenged to their highest and best."

With a few more words of encouragement, Mrs. MacDonald finished her talk.

"Seems like a pretty rugged way to hook a boy,"

remarked Susan dryly. "I'd rather have the sex appeal. It would be a lot easier."

"Yes, but you heard what she said the results would be," Anne chimed in.

"But I don't want to be an old maid. I know of some happy teen marriages. After all, getting married is the most important thing in life, especially for a girl."

"I'm not so sure about that," disagreed Jan. "I'd like to finish college and see the world before I settle down."

"Not me," said Susan. "I do want to finish high school, but my mom wants me to be popular. She thinks it's a disgrace if a girl isn't going steady by the time she is a senior."

"Not mine," said Jan. "My mother didn't marry until she was older. She had her fun first and wants me to date, but not to go steady. She's always warning me about getting serious before I finish school. She didn't date much in high school, but had lots of fun in college. I admit, it is hard to wait, besides you heard what Mrs. MacDonald said."

"What more is there to do in life, but get married?" Susan challenged.

"Heaps more," Jan answered quickly. "It is a matter of what you want to do *with* your life."

"I want to get married and have a family."

"That's wonderful, but what do you want a family for?"

"I don't know what you mean. I love babies, and I want somebody to love me. I can't wait to leave home and have my own place. Come on, Jan, don't you want to have someone who loves you?"

"Sure, but I think there is more to life than love."

"What?" challenged Susan.

"I can't answer you, but let's go ask Mrs. Mac-Donald. Let's ask for a question and answer time. I want to know some other things too."

Mrs. MacDonald was pleased to see the girls were doing some thinking. Saturday evening was set aside for answering questions.

Serious thoughts were laid aside as the girls were caught up once again in the fun of winter sports. Some of the lake had been shoveled for ice skating, and the cold crisp air added zest to the afternoon's outing. The girls came in for supper with blazing cheeks and hearty appetites. Could anything have tasted better than thick chunks of roast beef with mashed potatoes and gravy?

"Oh, my diet," groaned Susan, "but I'm starved!"

"The food's too good — I'm skipping my diet until I get home." Anne tried to comfort Susan, "There'll just be more of you for Bob to love, Sue."

"But you don't know. He hates fat girls!" moaned Susan.

"You're not going to get fat just over a weekend."

That evening the girls eagerly gathered around the huge fireplace for the answers to their questions. Mrs. MacDonald and Carol, one of the counselors, were to do the answering.

Mrs. MacDonald read the first question. "'How would the values a girl has make a difference in her life at home and at school?'

"When a girl gives her life to God, she values His way for her. At home this means having an attitude of love and respect for her parents. It means accepting them from God and doing her best to understand, obey, and help them. At school it means working hard to develop all her God-given capacity. A girl would then seek those things which are for her highest and best. Time-wasting activities would have to go. Value would be put on doing her best in school. Close friendships would have to be uplifting. In other words, a girl would begin to grow in wisdom and stature and in favor with God and man!"[1]

A hand went up in the back of the room.

"Does this mean we can have only Christian friends or friends from our own church?"

"Not necessarily — *close* friendship should be based on the standards and character of the girl. If your close friends have standards that are lower than yours, they tend to pull you down, rather than your standards pulling them up. But you should be friendly with everyone. Your friendliness can be an encouragement to many."

The next question was: "If God created sex to enjoy, what's so wrong about it?"

"Sex, like many other things has two sides. For instance, appetite is good, but gluttony is bad. Sleep is good, laziness is bad. And so God created sex pure, good, and lovely and to be kept in the right place. He made the attraction between men and women because He wanted them to marry and have children, but he did not create sex to be experimented with or played with outside of marriage.

"Sex is only one part of life, a very important part in adulthood. However, it can be a destructive force

[1] Luke 2:52

which leads to many a tragedy when not kept within the safeguards of marriage.

"Sex was planned by God for the enjoyment of husband and wife, and to enable them to have the joy of a family. When there is deep love and respect between them, a husband and wife are drawn together in the most meaningful of all relationships God has given.

"Question number three: 'How does a girl control a boy on a date? Won't a boy quit dating a girl who has standards that are too high?' "

Mrs. MacDonald asked Carol to answer this question. She hesitated a moment and then began.

"I'm a very lucky girl because I have a brother and we talk a lot of things over. He has told me how the fellows feel about the girls they date. They like girls who make them feel comfortable, ones who are nice to everybody and don't pretend they are something they aren't. Bill has been dating a girl lately who is a lot of fun. He said she isn't afraid of acting silly — not the kind of silly that makes a fool out of a boy, but one who loves to walk in the rain, run through puddles, and doesn't mind getting her hair messed up."

"Say, that doesn't sound so hard," Jan muttered to Lucy. "How is it some guys aren't racing after us eligible, charming, genuine girls? It looks to me like a lot of guys go for the girls that will neck and pet."

"Bill says that fellows want a girl who keeps her standards high without acting too goody-goody," continued Carol, "even though they may give the impression on a date that they want the girl to give in to them, they really don't respect a girl who does. No Christian fellow wants a girl who has been handled by every fellow she has dated. He wants a girl he can trust, who has kept herself pure, one who has self-control when his control may be faltering. A fellow looks to the girl to hold up the standard.

"As for a boy dropping a girl because he can't get what he wants from her, any girl should be glad to have that kind of a boy drop her.

"Really, girls, when my brother told me about the temptations he has, I was glad I'm a girl! I was surprised, but some of our clothes, and the very way we walk, or sit close to them, makes it rough, even when they try to keep their thoughts pure. We girls are not affected that way. Fellow's clothes or their walk don't have much affect on us one way or the other.

"My mother and I are very close, and she has helped me to understand a lot of these things. She told me that boys are aroused sexually through the mind, whereas a girl usually responds to the touch. That's why you should plan definite activities when you date — something that will be fun, and occupy your mind. Plan to keep busy and avoid any occasion for physical intimacy.

"If a boy tries to get out of line on a date, toss it off lightly and keep out of his reach!

"This summer Steve and I are to be married, and I'm so glad I've been able to keep myself for him, because of course, he's the most wonderful fellow in the world!" Carol joyfully concluded.

"This fourth question is interesting. 'Isn't there more in life than just getting married?'" Mrs. Mac-Donald smiled happily as she began.

"God intends for men and women to marry."

(Susan looked triumphantly at Jan.)

"But God did not plan marriage as an end in itself. It is the uniting of two people to fulfill His eternal and worthwhile purposes. For example, when my husband and I were first married, we were so much in love that our world was ourselves. In time our self-centered love began to fail as we became more and more demanding of each other. I was stunned one evening when Phil left the house in anger — all because he wanted me to go out and I wanted him to stay home. When he returned, there was icy politeness between us.

"The next day I sought the help of a wise and happily married older woman. She was able to show me the self-centeredness of our love, and the lack of purpose in our lives.

"That night I apologized to Phil. He too was sorry. We had a long talk, then dedicated ourselves *together* for God's will and began to pray that He would show us His purpose for our lives. Now we keep open house for missionaries, are active in our church, and I have this extra fun of camp work.

"There are other questions, but you girls are tired. We have covered some pretty important ground tonight and should leave the rest for another time."

Mrs. MacDonald said good night to the girls and they drifted off to the cabins. There was no prolonged talking that night as the girls dropped wearily into their bunks.

Sunday came all too quickly.

"I wish we didn't have to go home today," remarked Susan. It has been such fun, and the talks have been so good. I wonder what's planned for this morning? I never realized that talking about these things could be so interesting," marveled Anne.

During the morning, Carol shared with the girls what it meant to her to live for Christ in high school. She had so much fun in school that the young people who didn't know her were amazed to find out that she was a Christian. "We thought if you were a Christian you couldn't have any fun," they often remarked to her. But Carol's fun was different. Some of the places the young people went to she didn't feel she should go, but on other occasions, when she felt it was right, she threw herself into the activity.

Between sessions the girls crowded around Carol.

"Did you ever feel like you were different and the only one who did as you did?"

"Yes, many times I felt left out and lonely, and if it hadn't been for my mother, I might have given up. But instead I began to look around for other Christian girls and then we entered into the Christian youth group at school. In fact, it was about to fold up and we revived it with the help of one of the Christian teachers. We began to pray for different kids and invited them to the group. We also found some good speakers and some of the kids we asked began to find the meaning of life as they continued to meet with us."

"Did you find it hard not to go steady?"

"Yes, I did, but I got a gang of girls together and we formed a 'Never Go Steady Club.' The idea came from my brother's 'Bachelor Club.' In order to have membership in it, the boys were not allowed to date the same girl twice in a row and the fellow who dated the most girls was president of the club! My brother would ask me about different girls because I used to complain to him about the nice girls who were never asked out."

"Isn't that a great idea! I think we ought to try that when we get back to school," said Lucy.

"How about it, Susan? Are you game?"

"I don't know. I like having someone I can depend on and I don't know what Bob would think of such an idea. Anyway, if he started dating other girls, I might lose him."

Carol put her arm around Susan. "I know just how you feel. I felt the same way. Then I put my life into God's hands. Even then it was a real struggle not to go steady with Dick. I was afraid I would lose him, but I felt that it wasn't right to get tied down so young, because I knew I should go on to school. He was a nice fellow too, but we talked it over and agreed that if we were meant for each other, we didn't have to worry.

"It was pretty hard to lose Dick — which I did — but I met Steve a couple of years later. Now, looking back, I can see how Dick and I were not really suited for each other, and the choice I had made at sixteen was very different from the choice I made at twenty-one. Steve and I were part of a large group of young people in our college church. We didn't let ourselves get serious until our senior year. Now I'm glad I waited. So many of my friends have dropped out of school, and some of my high school friends, who married so soon after high school, feel that they have missed something in life by marrying so young. And they have. It is wonderful to have finished our education, and now Steve is prepared for his life work."

Susan's eyes filled with tears. Home was not a

happy place and it was not easy to give up the one thing that seemed most meaningful to her at this time (she was nearly eighteen). Turning away from the rest of the girls and putting on her coat and boots, Susan started for a walk in the woods. A struggle raged within her. Her mother would not understand if she chose to go on to school, and how could she do it alone?

The girls could never understand the bickering and fighting in her home, and if she could be married, she would get away from it all. But what Jan had said kept running through her mind. What did she want a family for? Would her home be any different from the one in which she was raised? Would she be any different from her mother? Did Bob really care about a good wife? Did he really love her for herself? These were real and tormenting questions.

"I don't want to miss the worship service," she thought as she turned back toward camp. These meetings had been helpful. She had never before given such serious thought to the problems of life.

Susan slipped into a back seat. The singing had finished and Mrs. MacDonald was getting up to give her final word of encouragement to the girls. They would all be returning home in the afternoon.

"This weekend you've listened to many different ideas which we trust will help you. As you go home remember God must control your life. I know it isn't easy to put yourself into the hands of an unseen God. The Bible says in Psalm 34:8, 'Taste and see that the Lord is good . . . .' I can tell you from my own experience that He *is;* that His plan for your life is the only one that will bring real fulfillment.

"You can't know God until you *give* yourself to Him and let Him begin to show you His love, His miracle working power, and His infinite wisdom. He is the One who made you. He knows you better than you know yourself and He knows your needs before you do. *You can trust Him* to show you what is right for you.

"Each day you will be faced with choices in every area of life. Your life will be shaped by the choices you make. As you ask God and *expect* Him to work, He will enable you to make the right choices.

"Won't you commit yourself, your fears, your future to His perfect love and plan for you? Will you do it now?"

Mrs. MacDonald ended her challenging talk with a heartfelt prayer for each girl.

Before the service ended, Susan had made her choice. She had put her life into God's hands. She would tell Bob when she returned home.

"I'll ask my Sunday school teacher to pray for me, and to pray that God will open the way for me to go on to school. I do trust Him," she said to herself.

5

Understanding Your Differences

One afternoon on the bus returning home from school, Jan and Lucy were chatting merrily, when suddenly Karin interrupted them.

"Look, why do you suppose Marti is sitting all alone? She really looks beat." Jan was immediately sympathetic.

"She's always full of fun and has a gang of kids around her. Something must be wrong. Let's go over and ask her."

"Marti, how come you're sitting alone? What's the matter?"

"Oh, nothing. I don't feel like being with the gang today . . . Oh, well, I might as well tell you," she said as she saw the sympathy in the faces of her friends. "It's really Miss Ryan. She picked kids for the swim team today. I think I can swim as well as Barbara Miller, but she put me on the second team, and she said I could be the head cheerleader. Honestly, I think she just did that to make me feel good, because she doesn't want me on the team."

"Boy, is that ever unfair! I've always liked Miss Ryan," said Jan. "I never thought she was that kind of a teacher! You're one of the best swimmers, Marti. I think you *should* be on the first team. They ought to get someone else who can't swim to do the cheerleading; no use wasting *your* talents. I think we ought to get together and go see her. After all, we are Marti's friends. What are friends for anyway?"

"That's right," answered Lucy, always ready to help the underdog.

"But are you sure you're right, Marti?" Anne asked. "I don't think Miss Ryan is that kind of a teacher. She usually has a good reason for what she does, and she is fair. Let's ask her why Marti isn't on the first team."

Marti brightened up immediately. The prospect

of her loyal friends standing by her and caring so much made life worth living again.

After school the group gathered around Marti, and together they went to the gym. It was Friday and there was no swim practice, so they found Miss Ryan alone, checking her records.

"Hello, girls, did you want to see me?" She greeted them cheerfully.

"Miss Ryan, we want to ask you a question about the swim team." Jan spoke for the group as they looked from one to the other.

Miss Ryan watched the girls as she began to anticipate the problem.

"You know Marti is one of our best swimmers, and can beat any other kid in the school most of the time, Miss Ryan. We were wondering why you didn't put her on the first team? And why did you give her the cheerleading job that *anyone* could do? We think she ought to be on the first team."

Miss Ryan looked from one to the other of the girls with understanding and appreciation of their loyalty and concern.

"I agree with you," she said, "Marti is good enough for the first team. However, competitive sports don't depend only on the skill of the person. There's a lot more to it than that."

The girls looked genuinely surprised.

"You see, I put Barbara on the first team, even though Marti can swim just as well, because Barbara has one very *necessary* quality."

"What's that?" the girls asked in a chorus.

"Barbara has a very strong will to win. Marti

loves to swim and she swims well, but it doesn't really matter a great deal to her if someone else wins, does it, Marti?"

"Why, of course not. Everybody likes a chance to win, so it's okay if others win sometimes. I just love to swim, and we have such fun together at practice. Everybody makes such a fuss over you and everything — it's really exciting."

"You see girls, Barbara's temperament makes her especially suitable for competing. She hates to lose. She is challenged by competition, and she *really has* to win. This gives her an advantage, because every bit of her skill is used every time she races. It may be she even swims a little better when the competition is close.

"Cheryl is our star diver. It is not only because she is more skillful than the others, but she is particular about everything. The things she does have to be done just right. It's the way she is about everything. There is something in her makeup that makes her strive for perfection, so she practices every day until each little move is perfect. It really doesn't matter to Cheryl whether anyone else is in the competition; she would do her very best if she were alone in the room. That is the way she is — so she is especially suited for the diving events where winning depends on perfection rather than a competitive spirit.

"Do you see what I mean? You, Marti, are an excellent swimmer. You belong on our team and you can win for us on the second team. We need you because you are as good a swimmer as the others and they respect you for it. That's why I made *you* cheerleader. Don't you see? Your enthusiasm is very catching and can be of vital help to the team to spur them on for that last ounce of effort they need to win. Cheerleading isn't just any old job. It is a very important one and we have to have the right person for that too."

The girls listened in fascination to these ideas. Lucy's eyes were wide with comprehension.

"Oh, is that why you chose Anne to be the manager? Because she is so easygoing and all the kids like her?"

"That's right, Lucy, Anne has the special temperament that can look at things from everybody's side and really be fair. She has a way of knowing what the right move is and who would be best against the other team in each meet. That is the thing she is suited for and what she does best."

What a time the girls had on the bus going home that night.

"I wonder what I'm suited for?" Lucy asked the gang.

"For making everyone feel good, Lucy. You always have something nice to say to everyone. No one could have a nicer friend," said Jan as they stepped off the bus and headed into the drug store for a coke.

6

Chartered Bus

The 2:15 bell rang — the end of the eighth hour. Ten minutes later almost all of the thirty three members of the girl's swim team were crowding into the bus.

"Hey, watch where you're going!"

"That's my seat!"

"I'm hungry, wait for me. I'll be right back. I'm going to get something to eat."

"My cap! I can't find my cap!"

"My bathing suit is still wet from yesterday!"

"Hang it out the window."

"No, it'll freeze."

"Eek! what was that?"

"I told you it was wet! That'll teach you to watch where you sit!"

"I'm back. Anybody want a coke?"

"Ooh, how can you eat?"

"I'm scared."

"She's scared!"

Slowly the bus pulled out. Somehow Jenny's feet got tangled with Marti's out in the aisle.

"Come on, grow up! Honestly, you act like my little brother," snapped Jenny. Then in a different tone, "Do you know what my brother and sister do? They snoop through all my things — and my parents let them!"

"That's terrible! My brothers would never dare to do that!" Vicki answered in a shocked voice.

"Why not?"

"I don't know. I guess it's because we've been taught to respect each other's property, or something."

"A lot of help you are," Jenny responded glumly, and started to move away.

"No, wait," Vicki was thinking hard. "Listen, if your brother and sister snoop in all your stuff and wreck it, what's to stop them from doing it to other people's things, and public property and things like that?"

"Yeah, that's right," Jenny agreed. "They'll probably grow up to be juvenile delinquents!"

"Why don't you tell your parents what Vicki said? Maybe they'll make them stop." Marti seemed to have faith in Vicki's idea.

"You know, it might just work!" Jenny's bad humor disappeared and she began to move toward the back of the bus.

Vicki sighed, "You know," she remarked to whomever was listening, "I'll trade my sister for anything available. Age twelve, spoiled rotten, and no good at all."

"I thought you said you got along with your family." Anne looked surprised.

"I said my *brothers*. They're okay, but Oh! My sister! She's my parent's favorite, and she can get away with *everything*. Not only does she get away with it, but I get blamed for everything she does! No matter what anyone else says, they believe her. What can you do about *that?*"

"She'll never be able to manage on her own when she leaves home, unless she learns to take responsibility for herself and for her actions," put in Miss Ryan.

"No kidding. She can't even manage summer camp."

"Why don't you get your brother, the oldest one, he's seventeen, isn't he? — get him to talk it over with your mother." Miss Ryan continued. "Talk it over when your sister is in bed. Do it on a day when you haven't been blamed for her wrongs. Then your mother will know you and your brother are really worried about your sister." There were a few minutes of silence as the girls thoughts drifted to the problems each one faced in her home.

Then Janna spoke. "My mother is a grouch. She yells all the time. First she tells me to do something, then if I do it slow, she yells because I'm wasting time, and if I do it fast she yells that I won't do a good job. She makes me clean up her messes, but has a fit if I don't clean up mine." Janna was indignant over the injustice of it all.

"You know, Janna," Miss Ryan said, "the thing that bothers your mother is probably the fact that you can't do the work as well as she would like to have it done. Everyone has this problem when they start something new. It takes time and experience to become good at a job. You just keep trying and you'll improve as you go. It won't be long before you are over this hurdle and your mother will really be proud of the things you do to help keep your home neat and nice. You'll see her impatience melt away little by little as she sees how you are improving."

"It's just the opposite with me. My mother does *all* the work. She's always so busy I never get any time to talk to her."

"Cheryl, why don't you try working along *with* your mother. Then she'll have more time to spend with the family, and you'll probably find she really enjoys talking with you as you work together. I used to love working with my mother. I found her interesting to talk to, and felt that I really got to know her. She often said her work seemed so much more fun when she had company."

"Well, Miss Ryan, what do you suppose is the matter with my parents? They are forever telling me that I owe them everything, and I should work for them all the time to pay them back. I feel like Cinderella or something."

"Carey, that's awful!" Bonnie was shocked.

"I wonder, Carey," Miss Ryan answered gently, "if your folks just want to make sure you appreciate what you've received. If you make a point of thanking them for your clothes, and little everyday things like lunches and dinners, as well as the special things they give you, you may find their whole attitude will change. There is no one so nice to have around as a person who thinks of others and shows appreciation for what they do. Young people today think the world owes them a living and your folks are probably afraid you'll grow up like that too."

"You kids think you've got it bad! My folks never let me do anything. They won't let me drive, go to pajama parties, or ride in cars if a boy is driving, and they won't even let me date 'til I'm eighteen. And they never give me any reasons for anything. They just say 'No' and that's it!"

"Why don't you ask them why?" Angela suggested.

"Are you kidding? They'd kill me! And besides," Lisa added, "they never give me time. They change the subject when I bring it up. They figure I know it already."

"Maybe it's your tone of voice. Boy, do my mom and dad ever clam up when my brother starts arguing about the things he can't do. They have told him a million times, I bet, that they will discuss it with him if he will be calm and polite, but he always gets mad, and talks awful. I don't blame them. I wouldn't want to talk to him either."

"I guess I do get kind of mad sounding too, but

they are so unfair! Still, maybe they'd be nicer if I tried to be extra polite when we talk about it."

Angela sighed. "Well, at least you all go places together. We never do. I'd give anything to go camping like you do!"

"Hey, listen. I'll see if my mother will call up yours and invite your family to come with us when we go skiing after it snows. Then maybe our mothers can get together and talk about the things they let us do. Your mom might persuade mine to let me do more things, and maybe your family will begin to enjoy having fun together."

"Hey, is that Franklin? Wow, it's big!"

"Not *that* big. Our school is bigger."

"Can we leave our books on the bus?"

"My cap's got a hole in it, right on top!"

"That's okay, it doesn't keep your hair dry anyway."

"Two more points and I get my letter!"

"I hope they have good refreshments. I'm starved."

"We're here! Hurry up you guys."

7

Friends and Dates

The door burst open and Jan flung herself inside.

"Oh, Mother, I just *have* to talk to you." Her mother turned from the stove, glad that her daughter wanted to talk. Jan talked most of her problems over with her girl friends these days but Mrs. Sherwood had tried to keep the lines of communication open between them.

"Remember I told you about Don and how everyone in the school thinks so much of him? We're in the same Lit class and I've been walking down the hall with him on my way to Chem class. Mother, you won't believe it, but he passed a note to me in Lit this morning and he wants to take me to the school play. Oh, Mother, all the girls in school want to date him. He's a wonderful fellow. This is a chance in a lifetime . . ."

"What's your problem then?"

"Well, he's not a Christian. Oh, Mother, I asked him to call me tonight. I just couldn't turn him down right then. All the way home on the bus I was arguing with myself. 'One date doesn't mean I'm going to marry him. But what about the next fellow who might ask me out . . . Where will I start to draw the line?' But Mother, you don't know how hard this is. He's one of the sharpest boys in school . . . and, and,"

"I'm thrilled at the way you have thought this through, Jan. It takes a lot of courage to say 'No,' especially when the fellow is so fine in himself."

"Mother, how will I turn him down? I told him to call me because my Mother might not let me go. May I tell him you won't let me?"

"Yes, if that will help you out of a dilemma. But be sure to continue being friendly, especially if he is the kind of fellow who seldom dates. There is such a difference in fellows. Some you couldn't discourage with anything, but others seldom date, and their ego is shattered when they are turned down. It may be a long time then before they ask another girl. It certainly is a compliment he has asked you."

After supper, the phone rang. It was Don. There was some friendly chitchat, and then Jan told Don she would love to go out with him, but her mother felt she shouldn't.

"Is it because of your religion?" Don asked bluntly.

"Yes, it is Don," she answered honestly.

"Oh," said Don with real admiration in his voice. "See you at school tomorrow," and with that he hung up.

Jan collapsed in tears. "Oh, Mother, I wanted to go with him so much."

"Honey, this is the sort of thing that builds character. I know how hard it is now, but the day will come when you will be glad you did the right thing instead of the easy thing, especially when the man of God's choice comes along. He's going to be mighty glad he has a girl who has already learned to say 'No' to the good and choose the best."

A few days later Jan came home in her usual bubbly way.

"Mother, you know I told you how Don avoided me when I saw him after he had asked me for the date? I did what you said. I spoke to him like I always had, but either he wouldn't look at me or he'd just mumble something. It made me feel awful because we've been such good friends. But today he was different. After Lit I was headed for Chem class when I heard, 'Hi, Jan.' It was Don! Oh, Mother, it is so nice to be friends again."

"You know, Jan, I found a book on preparing for marriage that I think you would enjoy reading. This book[1] tells of the importance of defining your ideals now, while you are in your teens. The friends you choose will color your choice of the one true, important 'friend' with whom you will be living the rest of your life."

"I like lots of different people. I think it would be pretty tiresome to live with the same person forever and ever. But come to think of it, you don't seem to be tired of living with Daddy for such a long time," Jan observed.

"Well, honey, I was pretty particular about the one I chose, because I *knew* I'd be living with him for life," her mother smiled. "Grandmother was wonderful about showing me how to choose the right one. She pointed out the importance of the right kind of friends, the type that would be uplifting. It is hard enough to cope with the drag of the day — the insidious degeneration on every side, the tide of evil — without having friends that drift with the tide.

"Oh, say that reminds me. I had a letter today from your cousin, Debbie. She heard I was helping Mrs. Allison gather material for her book for teens, so she sent me some of her ideas. I'm sure you'd enjoy her letter. What reminded me of it was that she wrote quite a bit about friends. Aunt Marilyn has written me that there has been a real change in Debbie now that she is nearly fifteen. It is wonderful how much good thinking girls do in their mid-teens. The teenage period is pretty exciting, but the early teens can be hard to live through because it is a period of rapid physical and mental change."

[1] Jill Renich, *Preparing Your Children for Marriage* (Grand Rapids, Mich.: Zondervan Publishing House).

Jan picked up Debbie's letter and read it.

Dear Aunt Helen,

Mother said you are helping Mrs. Allison to write a book for teens, and you want my ideas about things that give us the most trouble.

One of my problems was picking the right friends. Proverbs 2:20 says, "That thou mayest walk in the way of good men, and keep the paths of the righteous." It's awfully hard to find good friends, especially Christian friends. Most everybody wants to be "somebody" in school. It's easy to be a "big wheel" if you hang around with the kids who are. But these kids often do things that I don't feel are right. I mean, they are freer and usually looser with their standards.

Even when you realize it's wrong to go along with these kids it's hard to break away. One thing I did to break away, was to pray and pray and pray. I think that helped me the most. ["I'll bet Aunt Marilyn was praying twice as hard as she was," thought Jan.] Another thing I did was to make friends with a girl from my church, and I started going around with her. The other friend said, "Boy, Debbie, are you ever getting odd." I told her that she might think I was odd, but I was living the way the Lord Jesus taught and that is the best way there is to keep from being odd. What I said made her mad, but she came back. One day she said to me, "Debbie, are you mad at me?"

"Not exactly," I told her, "but I just don't like your kind of fun anymore." Then I noticed the more I said things like that the more she respected me. But even though she respected me she didn't want to hang around with me. I never said anything harsh and I never fought, but after awhile these friends didn't bother with me anymore.

I think my greatest problem is the week before menstruation. Probably every girl who is normal gets upset easily and is tense and irritable. At least I know I am. When I was thirteen I didn't realize how miserable I acted toward my family. Every little thing that happened I made into a mountain. I still get upset at small things, but there are a couple of things that I do now to help myself.

One thing is, if I'm going to say anything, it will have to be nice, or I won't say it. Another is I block myself off from the family. I don't mean lock myself in a room, but I try not to get into any conversations so I won't get into an argument with the kids or my folks. I just sit back and listen. These two things have helped me be more bearable to live with.

In these two problems my mother helped a lot. (If it weren't for her, I wouldn't be a Christian.) She said to me one day, "Isn't it true if a mother and daughter are both Christians they should be able to talk things over with each other?" I said, "Yes," and then just sat there, but I felt like she was giving me lectures all the time, when she was only trying to help me. Now I see how much those "lectures" have helped me. When someone said, "Mother knows best," they were right!

Another thing I think is important is dress. You know, if a girl wears sexy clothes all the boys will try to see how far she'll go. Everyone knows boys size girls up by the way they look and dress. Girls can wear sexy clothes just to become popular, but it doesn't really work that way. The girls in my school who wear that kind of clothes are sort of looked down on. Naturally there are some kids who like girls like that so they do have friends.

I think a girl can hit a happy medium in her clothing. If she wears pretty clothes and nice styles, it doesn't matter if her clothes aren't the fad. Just as long as they suit her, she'll be attractive.

Good hair grooming is important too. It doesn't have to be done in the latest fashion to be accepted by the other kids. In my school kids don't care too much about hair styles "in fashion." They get a style that does the most for them, and they're twice as pretty as they would be in any other style. In all the hair-do books I read, it always begins by saying the most beautiful hair in the world is the hair that shines. So I keep my hair real clean and brush it a lot, and all the kids say it looks nice.

Well, Aunt Helen, I can't think of anything more. I know I didn't say too much, but I hope it helps.

Love,
Debbie

P.S. I could have said *a lot* more, if I were talking to you!

Jan put down the letter. "Has she ever changed! She didn't even mention boy friends! When I knew her, that's all she talked about."

"Maybe she has changed there too," Mrs. Sherwood suggested.

"Anyway, what we started to talk about was the importance of the right kind of friends and forming the right sort of ideals for marriage. You probably won't marry any of the boys you know now, but you'll learn from ones you select for friends how to recognize and evaluate character in boys. And you'll need that when you *are* thinking of marriage."

"But Mother, how will I *know* when the right one comes along? I've met a lot of nice boys at school. I can't say too much for the boys at church. Why is it that there are so many nice boys who aren't Christians, and the boys who are Christians are so uninteresting?"

"It may look that way to you now," smiled Mother, "but there really are lots. You'll find more of them as you grow older. There are many in Christian colleges, Bible schools and even in Christian groups in secular colleges or universities."

"How will I know when I meet *him*? How did you know? Does God somehow tell you or what?"

"For one thing, honey, it is a good thing to *start praying about your life partner long before you meet him*. You must ask God to keep your heart and mind free from involvement with the wrong person. If you wait until you are interested in a fellow, your emotions may overwhelm you and you may find yourself attracted to a fellow who is not right for you.

"There are certain character traits that you should expect to find in your life partner. It was these that I found in your father, so that it did not really matter whether he was tall, dark and handsome. But I got that thrown in too!"

"You sure did, Mother. All my friends think Daddy is so good-looking."

"But, honey, you know what? He wasn't nearly as good-looking when we married."

"He wasn't? How come?"

"When I married him, I knew he had the potential of becoming a very fine man, but he was still young. Through the years he has become what I saw and felt he would. More and more of his beautiful character became evident in his face. That is what makes your friends think he is so good-looking."

"I never thought of that," said Jan in surprise.

"There are *four good ways* to tell if the fellow you are going out with is the man you want to marry."

"You sure make it sound simple, Mother."

"It isn't hard, honey, but I have found few people who were trained to judge character or to know what to look for in a life partner."

"I thought the main thing was that you loved him and that he was a Christian."

"That's important, Jan, but it just isn't enough. You not only want a Christian, but you also want one who has really *dedicated his life to God.* You want a man who feels that the will of God is the most important thing in the world for him. He doesn't have to be a minister or a missionary, but he has to feel that whatever he is doing is the thing that God wants him to do. There are too many people today who are half-hearted Christians and you would never be satisfied with that, Jan. Half-heartedness is apt to show up in other areas too."

"Like what?"

"Like his job, or his studies or even his home responsibilities. If he has the idea *anything* will go as far as being a Christian, he could carry the same idea over into his work and home life. You would never want that."

"As far as that goes, I'm sure that a fellow like Don takes *his* religion seriously and he's not half-hearted about anything, even though he's not a Christian."

"Yes, honey, but the trouble is that at the *heart* of your *life* you would disagree. Faith to him would mean one thing, and faith to you means something entirely different. It doesn't mean that a fellow isn't sincere either. He could be, but you just would not be able to go along with his ideas of faith and he would not be able to go along with yours."

"Don't you think I could pray and convince him my way is right?"

"That is not your place and that is the way many, many a heartache begins. If the boy is meant for you, you pray, but leave his heart attitudes with God. Many a fellow has changed for a girl until marriage, only to bring terrible grief to her later.

"I'm sure Don would never pretend to change."

"What you say of him leads me to believe Don *is* a wonderful fellow. It would be so easy to love a boy like him for his fine character, only to find later the heartache of having the core of your lives miles apart. But God also makes it clear that we are not to be 'unequally yoked.' "[2]

"Really, I know that you are right, Mother. What's another important qualification for a fellow I'd want to marry?"

"The second way to tell if the boy you are considering is the right one is to ask yourself if he stimulates you to your highest and best mentally as well as spiritually. This is a qualification I have heard few people mention when speaking of the important areas to look for in a life partner, but it is terribly important.

[2] II Corinthians 6:14

If you do not stimulate each other mentally and spiritually your life will end in a rut. You need to be challenged."

"What is the third?"

"The third is a similar background, that is, a similar cultural, national, and economic background. To marry someone from a totally different background adds more problems to the already existing adjustment problems."

"That doesn't sound very important."

"But it is, Jan. Our culture and background shape our basic attitudes toward the home, the children, and security. You will find that the fewer life differences there are between a couple, the better the adjustment will be. These differences can be great. Each one feels that his own particular background and culture patterns are right. Even though the partners are willing to adapt, often it means a change in their whole outlook on life. You don't think of all this in the first glow of love, but it is a very important consideration.

"The last qualification is love. Love must be based on character and not just on sex appeal. There will be some boys to whom you will feel strangely drawn. But keep your head. Ask yourself some questions: What sort of a person is he? Do you find it easy for your standards to slip a little, to compromise with your conscience, to give a little here and there? This could be infatuation. Infatuation is lust rooted in the sex drive. Infatuation must have and have now. Personal satisfaction is of primary importance, not the well-being of the one loved or the standards of God.

"Remember how all you girls were crazy about Doug?"

"How could I forget?" Jan laughed.

"You pointed out to me then that even though we didn't think much of him as a person, we just couldn't help being attracted to him. It's a good thing he *didn't* look at us.

"Real love is giving. It is self-sacrificing and subject to intelligent choice. Of course there is emotion, but it is controllable emotion. The control comes from high standards of conduct and practiced attitudes of self-control in other areas.

"In other words, honey, look for a fellow who wants God's best, who is intellectually stimulating to you, whose background is similar to yours, and is some one you can love with God-given confidence! Easy, isn't it?"

"Ohhhhh, Mother, do you think *I'll* ever find somebody like that?"

"Of course. My mother found my father in her generation. I found Daddy in my generation, and God is preparing a young man for you in your generation!"

8

Snap Judgments

It was a beautiful Saturday. The girls had decided to have a cook-out. It would be a wonderful change from school and something fun to do together. Jan supplied cokes, Karin brought buns, Anne potato chips and dip, Marti chipped in with the hamburger, and Terry brought pickles. Lucy suggested they invite the new girl who had moved into the neighborhood and was riding the bus to school with them.

"She'll probably be a drag because we don't really know her. Let's have her some other time," Jan suggested.

"But what other time?" Lucy asked. "You know we don't do this very often. It will be a good chance to know her better and to have her get to know us too."

"To be honest with you, I don't like her," Jan stated bluntly. "Her clothes and her hair are so extreme and she acts like she owns the world."

"I don't like her either," added Karin. "All she can talk about is boys and all the guys she dated before she came here and how fast they drove and the places she has been."

"She *is* a little different," admitted Anne tactfully, "But I really feel sorry for her. I think she is lonely and maybe if we got to know her we might find she's different from the way she is acting. She's probably trying to make an impression and this is the only way she knows how."

"I'm sure you're right," Lucy said eagerly. "Let's give her a chance. Maybe we could even help her," she added hopefully.

"I doubt it," said Jan, "but if the rest of you think we ought to have her, let's ask her."

Pam arrived at the picnic looking more like she was ready for a dance then a picnic at a park. The girls tried to hide their disdainful looks.

"Hi, Pam. We're so glad you could come," they greeted her.

"You're lucky I'm here," she replied jauntily. But her attempted nonchalance fell flat. Her whole manner was distasteful to the other girls.

"We wanted to get to know you better," Anne said quickly. "It is lonely coming to a new city and having to make new friends in high school," she added in her sincere and sympathetic way.

The girls watched Pam's face. A flicker of longing passed it.

"Oh, that's nothing. I'm used to making lots of friends. My dad has an important job, so we move nearly every year. I've been to twelve different schools and sometimes I've had to change schools in the middle of the year."

"Oh, Pam, that must be terribly hard," sympathized Lucy. "I've only been to three: grade school, junior high, and now high school. I'm glad my dad doesn't have that kind of a job."

"You get used to it," Pam said. It seemed to the girls there was a little wistfulness in her tone.

"What's the most interesting place you ever lived, Pam?" Jan asked, seeking to draw her out a little.

"Well, really, it was a long time ago," said Pam hesitatingly. She looked intently at the faces of the girls. Were they really interested or were they just trying to be nice? Did she dare answer the question honestly or should she laugh it off?

Lucy saw her hesitation, and beginning to sense her need, encouraged her. "Come on, tell us, Pam. You must have had lots of rough times too."

All of Pam's defenses seemed to melt away. A

soft light came into her eyes as she told them about a small town where she had lived and of her friendship with a minister's daughter. Often she would go home with Sarah after school and Sarah's mother took time to talk to her and seemed to love her. In fact Sarah's home was full of love and it spilled over to her. But that was a long time ago and since then she had made no close friends because it was so hard to leave the people she loved.

"But what about your mother?" Jan asked.

"Mother is never home . . . . Once I heard her say over the phone that she would be glad when I finished school and then I wouldn't be any more bother to her. I've tried to get jobs since then, but it's hard to when you're moving all the time. You keep hearing, 'Too young, no experience . . . ,'" she added bitterly.

"We're glad you're here, Pam. How would you like to fry the hamburgers?" Jan asked. Pam was delighted to have a part in the picnic.

"I've never done anything like this before with a group of girls," she told them happily. "This is fun." The conversation drifted on to activities at school and other things.

For Pam an afternoon had never passed so quickly.

"Say, Pam how would you like to come to our church party Saturday night?" Jan was not sure how the young people at church would take to Pam, but perhaps she could talk to some of them ahead of time, so they'd be sure to include her. "Come in sport clothes; you don't have to dress up for our crowd."

"I know, but this is all I have."

"You're just about my size," Anne said. "I have some extra things that I'd be glad to lend to you."

"Thanks, you kids are swell! I never knew any kids like you before."

"Perhaps you haven't given them a chance to know how nice you are," suggested Lucy.

"I guess I've been afraid that if they found out about my folks — my dad's drinking and all — they wouldn't have anything to do with me."

"My mother says it isn't what you come from that really matters but what you become," Jan remarked.

"We'll be seeing you."

Walking home from the park that evening, Jan had a lot to think about. It was *she* who had not wanted to include Pam. And then to have Pam open up as she did and to discover the unhappy home from which she came, made Jan feel badly. How foolish to have made such a shallow, quick judgment. Her folks often remarked that you could not judge by outward appearances. Her father had often rebuked her for "snap judgments," as he called them.

How could Pam even hold her head up in school? She must have a lot to her to do so well and without the help of Jesus Christ.

"I wonder what her father does that he goes from town to town," Jan thought aloud. She would ask Pam, if she had a chance sometime. Or maybe she'd better not. Maybe it would be better if Pam told her on her own. Perhaps his drinking had something to do with it.

That night at supper, Mr. Sherwood asked each of the children what the most interesting thing was that had happened to them during the day.

Rick told of the ball game he and his friends had

played in the park. He hit a home run and struck out only once.

Lyn had spent the day at her friend, Debbie's, and they had been working on a project for their science class.

"How did your day go, Jan?" her dad questioned.

"It was interesting," Jan answered, "and I think I have learned a lesson. You know how you have always told us not to jump to conclusions or to judge by outward appearances? You have been so right. Lucy wanted to include the new girl, Pam, who just recently came to town. I didn't like her, and I didn't want her to come, but we decided to ask her anyway. She came, all dressed up like she does for school. Her hair was just awful. It didn't look like she had combed it for a week. Anyway, we began to ask her about herself, and, Daddy, her life has been terrible. She has been to *twelve schools* and her mother wants her to hurry and finish school, so she can get rid of her! Here I thought she was really conceited, talking about boys and dates all the time, but I guess it has all been a cover-up. Now I feel dreadful for the way I have felt and talked about her."

"It is wonderful to have learned this lesson so young," said Mr. Sherwood. "Many people don't ever learn it. I think you will find that the fellows and girls who look and act extreme are often very insecure. They are longing for some of the attention that is missing at home. Usually it would take a lot longer for a youngster to open up than it did for Pam. She must have felt she was among friends or she would have kept up her front."

"What makes me feel badly," Mrs. Sherwood

added, "is that this judging attitude is even carried into the church. People are accepted or rejected because of clothes, money, or position and people's opinions about them. One of the ladies in church came to me recently and told me how she felt unaccepted because she couldn't and wouldn't 'keep up with the Joneses.'

"It is a wonderful thing, Jan, to learn to accept everyone and to look beneath the surface. You will find in the heart of most people the desire to do what is right, but they often don't know how."

"This has really changed my attitude," reflected Jan. "I've been thinking of other kids at school that I've avoided, because I didn't like their looks."

"They are the ones who really need someone to be friendly to them. Why don't you plan to ask some of them to church or to the Christian youth organization at school?" suggested Mr. Sherwood.

"I could do that, couldn't I?" Jan answered as she began to clear the table, absorbed in thought.

9

Health and Habits

There was a buzz of interest in the Homemaking room before class.

"Say, Anne, did you hear we were having a special speaker today?" Susan asked.

"No, I wasn't here yesterday. How come?"

Mrs. Smith is bringing a nurse in to talk to us about health and habits. It should be an interesting change," Susan added.

The class quieted down as Mrs. Smith came in with her guest. "I'm sure you girls will be interested to know that Mrs. Reynolds was a member of this class not so long ago. It probably isn't hard for her to remember just how she felt when she was in high school. I imagine she can remember the problems she faced. I might add that it wasn't too easy for her to go into nursing and get her college degree after high school. However, she didn't wait long after college to marry and now she is the mother of a darling little boy."

Mrs. Reynolds stepped to the front of the room looking from one girl to another as she began to speak.

"You don't know how interesting it is for me to have the tables turned and to be the guest speaker instead of listening to one. Never did I dream, when I used to attend this class that one day I would be standing here, speaking. Better watch out," she said with a laugh, "one of you girls will be doing the same thing one of these days.

"While dressing this morning, I thought about you girls. Some of you would be scrambling into your clothes; some of you would be searching madly for that belt you were sure you had hung up with your dress; others would be hurriedly pressing a blouse to wear. And still others of you would find you didn't have a clean thing!" The girls laughed as each one could see herself.

"When you got downstairs you gulped some juice,

or grabbed a piece of toast, or maybe you didn't feel hungry and are here with no breakfast at all!

"How do I know? I did the same thing — of course! All that my mother said was of no avail, so she finally gave up on me.

"Little did I realize then that all of the slip-shod habits I'd fallen into would make it hard for me to adjust to the rugged routine of nurses training. Some of the girls who started out with me just couldn't make it because of their poor health habits and their lack of discipline.

"It is easy to slop through life, but you young people need to realize that these are formative years. You can either build strong healthy bodies for the future, or you can drain yourselves of the vitality that you will need as adults. I have seen how hard it was for some young mothers to get back on their feet after childbirth because they were not able to recover the health they dissipated during their teen years.

"Life lived in a worthwhile way is not easy, and I'm not here to tell you it is! But I believe each of you wants to make the most of life. Habits are only one area of life, but a *very* important one. It will take a lot of thinking and a lot of determination on your part to stick to the things you feel you *should* do and *do* them.

"One important factor in health and happiness is adequate sleep."

The girls groaned. "Who wants to *sleep?*" they muttered.

"Do you wake up feeling refreshed in the morning or are you dragging halfway through the day? Generally speaking, adults need about eight hours of sleep. Some need more and some can get along well on less. Young people in the growing-developing stage should average at least nine hours a night.

"Continued lack of adequate sleep allows the accumulation of fatigue, which drains the energy and vitality you need to grow properly and to resist illness.

"Proper diet goes right along with sleep as an essential to good health. I'm sure you have studied the basic foods that should be included in your diet each day. Who would like to name them for me?"

Several hands shot up. Mrs. Reynolds pointed to one of the girls.

"Milk and milk products, whole grain cereals and bread, fruits and vegetables, meat or meat substitutes, fresh green vegetables like lettuce, citrus fruits for Vitamin C and potatoes."

"Good, I see you have learned *something*," Mrs. Reynolds said smiling brightly. "I wonder how many of you eat that way every day? How many here have cokes for breakfast?"

The girls shifted in their seats and grinned sheepishly. Mrs. Reynold's merry laugh rang out.

"All joking aside. It takes determination to eat properly balanced meals, instead of filling up on all sorts of sweets! I do believe there is an increased craving for rich foods at your age, but this is the time to establish good eating habits. It will pay off now in a lovelier figure and a clearer complexion and the pep and energy that come from good health. And later on, when you are not as active, you'll be better able to keep your youthful figure.

"Many of you are having a real problem with your complexion now. Plenty of outdoor exercise and a diet that is low in rich foods are good remedies for this. There is another important factor, though, and that is cleanliness. It is so easy to go to bed without washing your face. But girls, it is terribly hard on your complexion to have the grime and the makeup of the day rubbed in while you are sleeping!

"You should acquire the habit of soaping and washing your face and neck each night. Often, another good cleansing or two during the day are essential in combating the effects of excessive oiliness and cosmetics during the adolescent years. A healthy complexion needs little extra coloring. If makeup is used, it should not look artificial, but it should enhance your own loveliness."

"Many times the problem is complicated by your body's chemical changes during menstruation. Your doctor will be able to recommend a good covering cream to keep you presentable until you have won the battle with your skin.

"Your daily bath, and the use of a good deodorant will help you to fight the increase in body-odor during this period too. Be *very* scrupulous about this, as it will not only contribute to good health and looks, but it keeps you 'nice to be near'! Remember to make sure your clothes (especially your undergarments) are as clean as you are! The little effort of sudsing them out each night is well worth the time it takes."

The girls were taking notes. "It's *so* much to remember, and anyway, it seems like you wouldn't have time for anything else!" muttered Linda.

"This seems like a big order doesn't it?" sparkled

Mrs. Reynolds. "I *told* you it's not easy, but it *is* worth it!

"Your hair must be kept clean and shining by shampooing weekly and by lots and lots of good hard brushing every day. If you are afraid it will take out the curl, do it before you set it at night.

"A lot of work goes into any good product, and you'll find that every bit of time and effort you have invested in yourself will pay off in a more worthwhile, more useful, and productive *you* in the end. When you know you are at your very best, you will feel better, be more confident, more relaxed, and enjoy yourself more in any situation.

"There's one more thing that you will need to finish off this perfect package that is *you*. That is your 'wrappings' — your clothes. This is a little out of my field, but since this is a homemaking class, I'll just add a bit on that subject before closing.

"Your natural loveliness can be enhanced when you find the colors that suit you the best. You have no doubt already heard your friends say, 'Oh, Mary, I love your dress. Your eyes look so blue today,' or 'Jean, that red dress really looks sharp on you.'"

"You don't need to stick to that one color, but it is good to find your best color and build around it. There is quite a difference between style and fashion. Fashion changes with the times and seasons. Some fashions are nice and others are outrageous. There is no need to follow fashion. Style is something that particularly suits you. Tall girls need to wear clothes that minimize their height, and if they are slender they must avoid looking skinny. Heavy-set girls, by choosing the right colors and style, can look much more slender. There isn't time here to go into all of this. You can get books on the subject at the library. Often your mother will know why something doesn't look well on you.

"Be sure your clothes are neatly pressed, sparkling clean, and not in need of mending, and the hems are the right length!

"Thank you for listening so intently and looking so interested! It has been a joy to be with you. You will find that the older you grow the better life becomes. However, a rich and rewarding life tomorrow is built on self-control and good health habits that begin today."

10

Just for You

The girls were chatting happily on their way home from school. Most of them were pleased now to have Pam in their group. As Pam began to feel more and more accepted, her appearance began to change. Even though her clothes were limited, she was able to tone down what she had to wear. Even her voice was quieter so that it was no longer embarrassing to the girls.

"Oh, Pam, I almost forgot. There is a special meeting at church Sunday night for the young people. We're having a couple come to the church who are going to talk to us. I thought you'd be interested. The man is going to talk to the fellows and his wife is going to talk to the girls. Could you come with us?" Jan asked. "I'm sure my mom won't mind picking you up."

"I didn't know you had special talks in church! It sounds interesting and I'd like to go with you. My mother never cares what I do at night," Pam added.

Jan was glad for a chance to invite Pam to church. She had been waiting to ask her to something she thought would interest her. Pam had shown no interest in spiritual things when Jan had talked about the church at different times or had given her views on various subjects which pertained to her faith.

Pam was surprised at the number of young people who were attending the meeting Sunday evening. There was a friendly atmosphere in the group and several of them came over to speak to her. Jan had prepared the way for Pam by reminding the young people of her need to feel welcome. They knew how much the friendship of the group meant. They made her feel at home, including her in their happy Christian life.

They sang a hymn and then the boys went to another room to listen to Mr. Terry.

Mrs. Terry caught Pam's interest immediately by her warm, friendly manner and her delightful, charming smile. Pam liked her vivacious way of speaking.

"There is no subject I would rather talk about than marriage," Mrs. Terry began. "It is something I am now enjoying to the full, though it was not always this way. I had a great many things to learn when I married, and as I look back I see that I was inadequately prepared for this important part of my life.

"Little did I think before I married what it would mean to keep house, cook, wash, do dishes, dust and clean every day. Real homemaking is an art. It takes study, practice, and a disciplined life to keep a lovely home — even if it is just one room. It takes careful management too, to run a home on a small income. Not many people start married life with lots of money!" she chuckled.

"Nevertheless, a Christian marriage is something permanent and binding. You can change a job when you tire of it, but a marriage is for life, and the wedding ceremony says 'for better or for worse.' It can be better and better, but you will find that it does not come from just hoping so! How does it come? What makes a marriage better and better as the years go by?

"The first thing you will need for your happy marriage is a husband," Mrs. Terry's irresistible humor broke through. "You should be thinking about the kind of man you want for your life partner. Why don't you write a description of him? When I was in high school I did. He had to be six-foot-three, have brown eyes, black hair, and love children. It was very important that he be tall, dark, and handsome!

"As I grew older I began to realize he would need to have something behind his good looks. The kind of person he was became far more important than good looks. I started to look below the surface. When you begin looking seriously at a boy, ask these searching questions: Does he have the inner qualities that would make him a good husband and father? Is he willing to work, or does he feel that the world owes him a living? Does his conversation show his mind and thoughts are clean and uplifting? Is he honest and straightforward? Is he respectful to his parents? Does he honor them? Is he considerate of his sisters? Does he have the same basic outlook on life you do? Is he completely dedicated to Jesus Christ and His will?

"To many young people, love and security seem to be all there is to marriage, but remember, you'll be living with this man for a long time. Be choosy. You want the very best that God has for you. Look carefully for the character traits on which you can build a solid marriage and a happy home.

"Then you need to ask yourself some questions. Have you the qualities that would draw the best out of a young man? Are your thoughts uplifting, centered on how you can grow in your Christian life? Are you unselfish? The most important ingredient in marriage is unselfishness, and unselfishness worked in the heart by God. This is the basis for the deep love that enables a wife to adapt to her husband. Love that doesn't peter out when the first test or quarrel comes. In the ideal marriage there is one hundred per cent giving on the part of *both* husband and wife.

"Remember, though, you are not going to change magically at the marriage altar from a self-centered young girl into a beautiful, unselfish wife! Unselfishness must begin now. It starts in your home with your attitude to the other members of the family. Are you kind? Do you cooperate without grumbling? Are you training yourself to do the things you ought to do, not just the ones that you enjoy? Your training for marriage begins as you learn and perfect the skills of homemaking in your own home, and as you practice attitudes of generosity and thoughtfulness toward others, especially the members of your family.

"Do you enjoy children? Are you prepared to mold a little life for eternity? Are you developing patience and self-control to train a child in Christian character and lead that little one to Jesus? One of the sweetest joys in life is that of leading your own precious children to the Lord Jesus Christ.

"Your prayer life is an important part of your contribution to marriage. Do you spend time now every day in prayer? Is God answering your prayers? Can others depend on your prayers? Are you growing in your Christian life?

"Do you put a high value on yourself? Have you thought through the standards you will hold? The Bible says it is not good for a man to touch a woman outside of marriage. Fellows and girls are to keep their embraces and kisses for marriage. Save yourself completely for your life partner. Set your standards at God's level, and stick to them. Once you let down, each kiss or embrace will make it easier for the next one, and the next. You begin to make excuses. Your conscience becomes dull, and your standards drop. Keep your standards at the highest level.

"When the right boy comes along, he will have an invaluable girl, a girl whose price is 'far above rubies.'[1] *That* boy will have a right to be proud of his fiancée!

"To sum it all up, it takes a mature person to build a happy and worthwhile marriage. Here is a check

[1] Proverbs 31:10

list for you to find the areas where you still need to grow and develop before you are ready for this wonderful adventure:

                                                    Yes No

1. Am I preparing to be a good wife?
2. Am I living unselfishly at home?
3. Do I control my temper?
4. Do I get along well with members of my family?
5. Do I like to earn the money for my personal things and my future education?
6. Do I behave discreetly around boys?
7. Do I live within my budget (allowance)?
8. Does happiness in marriage include love for a home and children?
9. Am I considered self-controlled and able to profit from criticism?
10. Do I stick to my high standards in spite of what the crowd says or does?
11. Do I do things for others instead of just expecting them to do things for me?
12. Am I growing in my Christian life?

"There are many, many things I could share with you; I've mentioned only a few of them. I will feel it has been worthwhile if I have encouraged you young people to do some serious thinking about your responsibilities as you consider marriage and homemaking."

At the end of the talk the girls were quiet and

thoughtful. Most of them had not thought beyond the point of being loved and cared for. They had not given thought to their responsibilities in marriage.

"Mrs. Terry, do you believe that God wants *everybody* to get married?" one of the girls asked earnestly, and much to her embarrassment, the other girls burst out laughing.

"I believe that marriage is God's plan for most of us. There are those of course who do not marry, but on the whole God intends for most of us to marry and to bring children into the world for His glory.

"However, there are a lot worse things than not getting married!" she added with an infectious laugh. "To those who find His will, God gives great joy and satisfaction in the work He has called them to do. I know of women who love their work and do not want to marry. Of course, I'm so happy I'm prejudiced. I want all of you to find the best man in the world — to be his companion in serving God and to share the joy of children growing up in your home to be trained for the Master's service.

"Perhaps another time we can talk more about the love and courtship side of life, but I think this is enough for now. I hope this has given you something to think about."

11

Bible Party

Monday Pam joined the girls at the bus stop.

"Hi ya' kids," she greeted them.

"Say, Jan, that lecture last night sure wasn't anything like I thought it would be. I thought you just talked about God or the Bible or something — "

"That *was* sort of special, Pam, but I'm glad you liked it." Jan was pleased. Pam had said little last night when the Sherwoods drove her home. It had been hard to tell what she thought.

"You see, Pam, the Bible tells us how we should live. Once in a while we have special speakers like Mrs. Terry or a missionary who tells us about her work, but what I think are the most fun are our Bible Parties."

"Bible parties! What's that? How can you have a party with the Bible!" Pam was surprised.

"Here comes the bus," one of the girls announced.

"Here, sit with me, Pam, and I'll tell you about it on the way to school."

The girls pushed their way to the back of the bus where they found an empty seat.

"Lucy, Anne, and I always try to start each day with Bible reading and prayer," Jan began.

"How come?"

"Because we want to do God's will every day. If we don't read His instructions . . . ."

"His instructions? What's that?" Pam interrupted.

"The Bible, where He wrote down what He wants us to do."

"Oh," said Pam, still a bit mystified.

"Anyway, we read the Bible and that's God talking to us. Then we pray and that's us talking to God."

"You — talk — to God?" Pam had never heard of anyone her age who talked to God. She thought it was just ministers who did things like that.

"Sure," Jan answered, finding it hard to realize how foreign these things were to one who had never known God personally nor known faith as a way of daily living.

"Anyway, as I was saying, we try to read our Bible and pray each day, although sometimes the Bible is hard to understand."

"You mean the Bible *isn't* just for preachers?"

"No, it's for everyone."

"Everyone? Even kids? I'd hate to have to read it."

"It isn't *that* bad, Pam, but some parts are kinda hard to understand and the parts between the stories are kinda boring."

"I'd think so."

"Now this is what I'm getting to. We kids decided to talk to Mrs. James. She used to teach our Sunday school class. She was a wonderful teacher and made us love the Bible. Anyway, she gave us a neat idea so the Bible'd be more interesting."

"What was that?"

"She suggested we get a modern version, like Phillips' New Testament[1] or *Living Letters*[2] and then read and mark our Bibles with different colors."

"*Mark* your Holy Bible! Isn't that a sin?"

"Oh, no. It's Holy because it's God's Word, but when we mark it, Mrs. James explained, it makes it more personal to us.

"For example, commands you mark with red. The Bible says, 'Love one another.'[3] That verse you underline in red — and boy, did that get me, when I hated Barbara. I saw I was disobeying *God!*"

"Then, promises are marked in blue. Like, 'Fear thou not; for I am with thee.' "[4]

"Wow, I've never heard of such a thing, but it sounds interesting."

"There's lots more to it — I mean other colors 'n things, but it'll take too long to explain right now.

"Anyway, all of us mark our Bibles at home, but it makes it lots more fun when we meet together and compare notes. That's what we do at our Bible Parties. We bring cokes, chips and dip, and sit around on the floor reading and marking our Bibles and talking over the verses together. It's really fun. We'd love to have you come to our next one, Tuesday, at Lucy's house."

"I'd love to come, if you don't mind, and if I didn't like the party, at least I could eat!" Pam accepted laughingly.

[1] The Macmillan Company, New York, New York
[2] Tyndall House, Publishers, Wheaton, Illinois
[3] John 15:12
[4] Isaiah 41:10

Anne and Jan stopped by for Pam on their way to Lucy's.

"We have an outline we go by. It's a guide that makes our studying the Bible easier and keeps us to the point a little better. When we start our study we'll give you one and you can use it at home too, like we do."

As the girls settled themselves on the floor in the den at Lucy's, Pam poured over the guide Mrs. James had prepared for them:

COLORED PENCIL BIBLE STUDY

Light Obeyed — Increaseth Light

Light Rejected — Bringeth Night

Commands to heed . . . . .Promises to encourage

Read and mark your Bible as follows:

Commands — Red

Promises — Blue

Challenging statements — Green

References to the Holy Spirit — Gold (Yellow)

Warnings — Black

Words which stand out to you—like: all, love, believe, etc. — in the verses studied, mark over with your other colors.

Study Guide

  I. Select a book of the Bible (try James or Philippians if you don't know where to start).

 II. Read a chapter (or a few verses if time is short) and underline the verses as instructed above.

III. In a notebook answer the following questions:

  A. Are there any commands?

    1. Do they, or could they, apply to you?

    2. If so, how? Take one at a time. Describe.

B. How do the promises apply to you? (Write about each one separately.)

C. Are there any statements that challenge you? How?

D. What new thing have you learned about God the Father? Jesus Christ, His Son, our Saviour? and the Holy Spirit in this chapter?

E. If there are any warnings, what can you learn from them?

F. Do any words repeatedly stand out to you? Which ones? What emphasis is God making by this repetition?

"The study is so interesting we don't get many verses done at one time, Pam. We've been studying James together most of the winter and have only come to chapter four, verse eleven," Lucy explained. "Jan, you read what it says in *Living Letters.*"

"Don't criticize and speak evil about each other, dear brothers," Jan read. "If you do, you will be fighting against God's law of loving one another, declaring it is wrong. But your job is to obey the law, not to decide whether it is right or wrong."

Pam was amazed as the girls shared thoughts on the wrong of criticizing one another. They remembered how they had criticized Mary Beth, one of their classmates. After she left school a teacher had shared with them her struggle to make the grade while caught in a law case between her parents.

Lucy read from the same verse in Phillips, "Never pull one another to pieces." You see, Pam, that's a command from God and we underline it in red. If we really love people as God would have us, we'd never pull anyone to pieces, like we did Mary Beth."

As the girls read on about judging one another and the right and wrong attitudes toward planning for the future, Pam became more and more interested. For the first time she began to see an unusual depth in these girls who had become her friends.

At the close of the Bible study the girls prayed for themselves and their friends by name. They wanted to interest their friends in becoming Christians. They prayed for Pam.

Jan invited Pam to her Sunday school class and also introduced her to Mrs. James. It seemed unusual to Pam for a lovely married woman to be so interested in girls — their problems as well as their joys.

One day Pam asked to visit Mrs. James. She found her so easy to talk to. Even though the girls had been wonderful, she was reluctant to share everything with them.

"Mrs. James," Pam began, "I'm kinda mixed up. I've been going around with Jan and the kids all spring. Those kids are different. They make me feel like a crumb," she said earnestly.

"I'm sure they don't mean to, Pam."

"Oh, I don't mean it that way! They're swell kids, and have been wonderful to me. They never made me feel like they looked down on me — — but it's — — it's hard to explain what I mean. They won't cheat in school, they say that's stealing, and it's wrong. They try never even to *think* wrong things about the other kids! They say the Bible tells them to think only kind things. I'm not that way. Something seems to be missing in me. I feel real resentful toward my mother 'cause I think she wants to get rid of me. I'm ashamed of my dad. And I just hate those kids at school that think they're so hot! And what's *wrong* with cheating? Everybody does it. And, well, I feel awful. I want to be like they are, Mrs. James."

"You can be, Pam. God loves you, and He wants you to be full of His love too."

"But, Mrs. James, God doesn't love *me*. Lookit, I don't do the things He says to in the Bible, and I don't even *want* to, really. I'm not that kind of girl."

"What kind?"

"Well, good — like they are. You know. I'm bad inside, and, well, God wouldn't want *me*."

"There's where you're wrong, Pam. God *does* want you. But the sinful, wrong, selfish things in your heart are like a big wall that keeps God's love outside of you. This is what is wrong with the world. All of us are naturally just like you say you are. Everyone wants his own way. It's human nature to want to come out on top, to get angry and to hate people who are mean to us. This is what the Bible means when it says "all have sinned, and come short of the glory of God."[5] But God still loves us and He wants to reach us with His love. He wants to forgive us and to change us so that we are freed from our selfish ways.

"To make this possible God sent His Son, Jesus Christ into the world. The Bible tells how He lived a perfect life, then died for our sins, and then arose from the grave to be our Saviour. This is why we have Good Friday and Easter.

[5] Romans 3:23

"You cannot change yourself. Only God can forgive you and change you. But you can tell Him of your need. He wants you to give yourself to Him just as you are, and when you receive Jesus Christ into your life to be your Saviour and your Lord, He forgives you. He breaks the wall of selfishness so that God's love can fill your life and change you. That's what He did for Jan and her friends. *That's* why they are different.

"Would you like to ask Him to do it for you now?"

"Yes, I would, Mrs. James!"

"Let's just talk to God then, Pam. You tell Him everything you've told me."

The two bowed before God, and Pam said, "God, you see what I'm like, and I don't want to be this way anymore. I want Jesus to come into my life and make me the way You want me to be."

Then she read, "Him that cometh to me I will in no wise cast out,"[6] as Mrs. James directed her in the Bible.

"Did you come to Him, Pam?"

"Oh, yes!"

"Did He accept you?"

"I don't know . . ."

"What does He say?"

"He says He will."

"Then did He?"

"He must have," Pam said hesitatingly. "Yes, He did!"

"Then let's thank Him," suggested Mrs. James. "Just tell Him 'thank you' for keeping His promises, for

6 John 6:37

wanting you, and for taking you for His own from this minute on."

Pam began slowly and uncertainly to do as Mrs. James suggested, but suddenly her heart overflowed with thanksgiving to God for the wonderful love He had poured out on *her*. She didn't deserve it. She couldn't believe it . . . but she *did* believe it! and the joy and the happiness in her face made it radiant and lovely. She forgot Mrs. James as she poured out her heart to God about all the little and secret things she really thought. How she resented her mother, but really wanted to love her so much, and how she wanted her dad to be like other fathers so she could be proud of him. Her loneliness and anger at being snubbed, and her gratitude to her new friends for loving her. "But most of all, I want to do what You want me to do *all* the time, and I'm sure glad You are going to help me!" she finished happily.

There were tears in Mrs. James' eyes as she silently thanked God for making Himself real to Pam, and for Pam's simple, trusting acceptance of His love and forgiveness.

Pam turned to Mrs. James. "But, Oh, Mrs. James, I feel so unworthy!"

"You are, but He loves you and has been wanting you for a long time. Now *He* wants to make you worthy of being His child — the King's daughter!"

12

Gifts

"Say, Anne, tomorrow is Mother's birthday and I don't know what to give her. I spent most of my baby-sitting money, so I don't have much. Can you think of something cheap, but elegant?"

Anne laughed. "Now that *is* a problem. What do you think I am, a magician? I have enough trouble stretching my own allowance! But say, I read of a great idea in our church paper. Some girl wrote on separate cards things she would do for her mother. Then she put them in a box and gift wrapped them for her birthday.

"For instance, four of the cards said:

> Upon the receipt of this card
> I promise to wash dishes cheerfully
> for one day.

> Upon the receipt of this card
> I promise to baby-sit without
> complaint.

> This card promises the bearer
> a vacuum cleaning of all the
> house.

I will be happy to do all the
left-over ironing upon the
receipt of this card.

The other cards were similar."

"Anne, that's a wonderful idea. Mother can always use note paper and then I can wrap this other gift up too. It is a lot harder to give my time than to buy something, but that is what I'd rather do. Speaking of gifts, Anne, what sort of gifts do you think a girl should give a fellow? Maureen told me she was going to give Bill a sweater for his birthday."

"My mother says a girl should not give a boy anything that is personal, like clothes or expensive jewelry, and vice versa."

"What does that leave for a girl to give then?"

"Well, you could give him some knickknack like a key ring with a model of a car on it, if he's car crazy, or bake him some cookies, or make him a box of fudge, or buy him a good book. The gifts should be the kind that are more or less temporary."

"Gifts are sure a problem. It seems like I never have any money when it is time to get something for someone."

"I have the same trouble, but you know, it's really a matter of planning ahead, or not planning ahead which is just a bad habit. If we'd keep a small savings for unexpected expenses, we'd have money when we needed it. It sure is embarrassing to have to ask Dad for the money to get him a present! I've decided never to do *that* again! It looks like I'm going to have to get into the habit of saving some of the money I earn."

"Mother is pretty strict with us about our money. Out of everything I earn or from my allowance, I first have to take out ten per cent for the church like God commands.[1] Then, depending on the amount, I have to put at least ten per cent into my savings account for college or some other big thing, like my hope chest or a trip abroad. Then I'm supposed to budget the rest so that I can buy the things I need. But this is where I get caught. I find it hard to hold on to that money when I see something I want, even if I don't really need it."

13

Popularity

It was a beautiful spring day and the girls were going home from school. The bus was crowded with commuters and noisy young people. On the back seat a couple of high-schoolers were engaged in a warm embrace. Some of the riders looked on with interest; others turned away in disgust at the public display of affection. The crowded bus began to empty as it neared the edge of the city.

"My mother is terribly old-fashioned," Jan told the others. "She thinks girls in their early teens should only double date or group date."

[1] Malachi 3:10

"Mine doesn't," Karin added. "She wants me to be popular and have lots of dates. Guess she's afraid I'll be an old maid!"

"Why is your mother so strict, Jan? Why does she think girls in their early teens should only group date?" Karin asked.

"She told me, but it's hard to explain. I'll ask her again tonight. For one thing, she said girls who don't date until they are older have a lot more fun!"

"Why's that? A date's a date and would be fun any time. The sooner the better."

"Mother said that when a girl is older her standards of conduct are more settled. She is more confident and sure in her mind as to right and wrong. She can enjoy a date, be a lot freer in her attitude, and enjoys learning how a fellow really thinks and feels. Anyway, she said she didn't date until she was older and when other girls were taking dates for granted, she was having the time of her life."

"But that was in the old days. It's different today. Girls do things much sooner now than they did then. I don't think *that's* any reason."

"She did really have some good ones, but I'll have to ask her again. Anyway, look at Jack and Sandy back there. It gets worse every day."

"Yeah, but did you hear what Mr. St. John said in Chem class when we asked him where Mary was?" Lucy asked. "We'd been missing her in class this semester. He told us that she's not coming back to school . . . and you know why!"

"Not Mary!" all the girls echoed. "Why she's one of the nicest girls in class. She's not that type!"

"I know, but it sure makes you sick. I didn't even think she was going steady. She's not as old as I am."

The bus stopped to let the girls off. After going to the drug store for cokes, they separated for home. Each girl was wondering *why* it had to happen to Mary. She was so gentle and likable. None of the girls knew her well, but all in her class liked her.

Jan burst in the door at home. "Mother, Lucy just told me what happened to one of the girls at school and I feel just awful. If you only knew how nice she is, you would feel awful too."

"What happened?" her mother asked, setting aside the letter she'd been writing.

"Lucy said one of the girls asked Mr. St. John where Mary was this semester and he told the whole class she wasn't coming back, and implied she was going to have a baby! It's awful, and I don't think he should have told."

"Maybe he had a reason for telling the class."

"What reason could he have? He was just making it harder for Mary."

"Maybe he thought if he told the whole class it would make some of you do some thinking."

"But Mother, you don't know how nice Mary is, and I can't believe *she* would get into trouble."

"That is probably just why the teacher told you —just as a warning that it could happen to anyone.

"I'll never forget something your Dad and I saw one day. We were on a little vacation by Lake Michigan. It was a beautiful, clear, cold day in winter. The sand along the lake was frozen and deserted and we decided to drive along by the water to see how far we could go. A mile or two down the frozen beach we passed a parked car facing the lake. In the car was a young couple sitting side by side in a close embrace. After traveling up the shore a few miles, we found the beach blocked, so we turned around and came back.

"The car was still there when we returned and I glanced at the couple as we went by. The girl was no longer sitting beside the boy, but was on his lap.. She had on a beautiful pink sweater and looked like a lovely girl, but her face and actions showed excessive and uncontrolled emotion. The couple had gone too far. I'm sure they had not intended to when they began to enjoy the view, but they didn't know where to draw the line. They didn't know when to stop. They didn't know the power of their own emotions, and they didn't know how to handle them.

"Oh, honey, this can happen to anyone. But it is less apt to happen to a girl who has set her standards high and has learned to use self-control."

"Mother, is this part of the reason you don't believe in dating too young?"

"Yes. You see, the young teenager's body is just developing into womanhood. She has not had time to adjust to her adult emotions and sex drives. Her ideals are not fully formulated. Many girls at this age want to experiment with their bodies to see how it feels to be loved and kissed by a boy. But this is the time that she needs to exercise self-control and keep herself pure for the boy of God's choice for her. Group dating helps to keep the controls on (providing, of course, the group is of the right sort). This too is why we are so strict about not using a parked car for a sitting room.

"And, honey, another wonderful provision God has made for this difficult time is a tender heart toward God Himself. At this age young people want to dedicate their lives to Him, when the challenge is presented. This is why God asks you to give Him your body."[1] It is so easy to say, 'I'm a Christian,' and then live as you please, but it is another thing to realize your *body* belongs to Him — as well as your mind and heart.

"Perhaps, if Mary had realized that her body belonged to God, she would have been careful not to turn it over to her boy friend."

"Mother, I still feel awful about Mary. Do you think she should get married, or just have the baby?"

"That is very hard to say. She and her boy friend are just not ready to face life as a married couple. Neither have finished high school. Jobs are scarce as it is, and it will be very hard for him to find one that will support a wife and family.

"If Mary goes away to a home to have the baby and it is adopted out, she will always wonder, should she have married the boy? Would he have been able to support her? Did he really love her? Who has her precious baby?"

Sad at heart, Jan went to her room. Even though life was full of fun most of the time, there *were* problems. This *could* have been she, but it wasn't. A pure life was still before her — for what?

[1] Romans 12:1

Quickly changing into comfortable clothes, she went downstairs to set the table for supper. She was not her usual, sunny, chatty self. During supper the family noticed her quietness.

"What's the matter?" asked Rick innocently, "flunk a test today, Jan?"

"No," she answered quietly.

"Then why are you so quiet?" Rick persisted.

"Just thinking."

"Oh, then you must have a headache," he laughed.

After supper Jan went upstairs to study, Rick ran off to play, Lyn stayed to help with the clearing up, and Dad buried himself behind the newspaper.

"Say, Jan," he called to her later, "can you come down a minute? There is something here in the paper I think may interest you.

Jan came downstairs and looked over her father's shoulder.

STARTLING FACTS YOU SHOULD KNOW

DISEASE . . . Complete figures would show that about 200,000 teenagers contact a venereal disease each year in the United States.

U.S. Department of Health, Education and Welfare, 1962.

One-fourth of all reported infectious veneral disease in the United States involves persons under 20 . . . . [Since 1959], primary and secondary syphilis increased more than 120 per cent in the under 20 age group — a greater rate of increase than in all other groups combined.

— *Ibid.*

DROPOUTS . . . Pregnancy and/or marriage were listed by more than 30 per cent of white and negro girl dropouts as their reasons for leaving high school, according to a 1962 study by the Maryland Department of Education.

"I know, Dad. One of the girls in my class dropped out of school this semester because she is having a baby. I told Mother about it. Isn't there some way kids could be helped before it is too late? You and Mother have talked to me and it has all helped so much, but what can be done for the kids who don't have this opportunity?"

"Why don't you suggest it to the youth director at church and see if he could arrange a series of meetings for teens. Someone who knows their problems could give a talk, or there could be a panel of people who work with teens. You could ask questions after listening to them."

"Oh, Daddy, that's a wonderful idea. I'll bet a lot of the kids from school and the other churches would like to come if we had a series of meetings like that!"

"Perhaps you could have a Christian nurse speak to you. I know of a Christian policewoman who'd be glad to speak to young people, if she could work it in . . . ."

"Thanks for your ideas, Daddy, I've had so many opportunities at camp, church, and home, but lots of kids just haven't had a chance.

14

Spring Banquet

It had been a long drab winter. It seemed as though spring would never come! But today was just beautiful. The trees were beginning to bulge with new life. Young people stood in clusters outside the church chatting between Sunday school and the morning worship service. Everyone looked so happy standing in the bright sunshine snatching a few relaxed minutes between services.

As the Sherwoods walked past the young people on their way to service, Jan disengaged herself from the group and whispered to her folks, "Do you mind if I sit with the kids today?"

"No, honey," her mother answered, "but don't forget you are in church."

"Oh, Muh-thur!" Jan exclaimed as she hurried off to join the young people.

After the service, the family took the long way home. It was such a lovely day, they all hated to go indoors. Jan could hardly suppress her excitement.

"You know, the spring banquet that several of our churches are having for the young people? It's going to be downtown at the Hilton in the Starlight Room, and guess what?"

"You have a date," Rick announced in a sing-song voice.

"How did you know?" challenged Jan.

"You oughta see your face — anybody'd know!"

"Mother, make him quit it," Jan begged, the light going out of her face. "Little brothers are sure a bother," she added glumly.

"Who is it? Who is it? Who is it?" begged Lyn, excitedly from the back seat.

"Never mind," said Jan sourly.

"But, honey, you brought up the subject. Let's not turn this lovely day into a quarrel," her mother interjected.

"I'll tell you later, Mother, but make the kids lay off, won't you?" Jan pleaded.

"Let's change the subject," Mother suggested. "Isn't it a beautiful day?"

"Look how bulgy the ends of the branches are," Dad pointed out. "The trees are getting ready to scatter their seeds and soon there will be millions of little seedlings coming up all over the place."

"It sure makes a mess to rake up," complained Rick, picturing the hours he spent trying to keep their lawn clean last spring.

Dad ignored Rick's complaint and continued. "Have you ever thought of the abundance of God? Notice the millions of seeds scattered, even though only a few produce trees. Have you ever seen the scores of seeds from each flower that are allowed to mature? It is thrilling when you think of how God pours out His blessings in the same way. So often folks think of God as stingy and trying to make life as hard for us as possible, but just one look at trees in the spring can change a thinking person's mind."

The day was so warm the family decided to serve their food from the stove and take it outside to eat at the picnic table. What a wonderful time spring is — a time for new beginnings — a time when God, somehow, seems closer.

It was a quiet afternoon. While the family rested, Jan and her mother cleared up the dinner things.

"Tell me about your date," Mother encouraged.

"It's so exciting, Mother. All the girls want to go out with Tim, and he asked me!"

"Who is Tim?"

"Don't you know, Mother? His family just moved here a few months ago from Minnesota. His dad is a designer or an engineer or something. Haven't you met his mother? She's the new choir member. Anyway, Tim's a doll, and so nice to everyone that all the girls are crazy about him. He isn't real tall, but he's awful nice."

"I'll look forward to meeting him when he comes to the house to get you."

"Then you can tell me what you think of him, but I'm sure you'll like him."

"Don't forget, Jan, it is up to you to help him enjoy his date with you. Between now and the time you go out, you'll have to find out his interests and study up on them! Remember to have at least ten different topics to talk about! Don't forget to draw him out and let him do a lot of the talking. There is nothing more enjoyable for a fellow than to be able to talk freely."

"I know, Mother. A counselor at camp told us how her brother likes girls who are lots of fun, but who don't make him look silly. How late can I stay out?"

"I know that after the banquet and concert you just *have to* go some place to eat. It seems to me an hour and a half after you leave the program should be enough time."

"We'll be going with Paul and Sharon. Sharon is a nice girl, but she loves to brag about how late she stays out on a date."

"Honey, don't try to compete with her. You know when we expect you home."

"I know, but I hate being the first to suggest we head for home."

"You may not like it, but you need to do what is right."

"Yes, I know, but no one else has to be in as early as I do."

"While you are in the midst of it, it is hard to realize that this is your training ground for the future. It is so much easier to *learn* to do what is right when you are young. It is much harder when you are older. Go along with the crowd now, and when you become a mother, you will be keeping up with the Joneses, instead of setting the standard and *leading* the way. You are a born leader, Jan, and if you start to follow the crowd now — I hate to think where you will be leading young people later."

"But Mother, what's the harm in coming in late, or should I say early in the morning? We're not going to get into trouble."

"I know you won't, honey, but it is just starting something that has no end. The later the hour, the more your resistance is lowered and you do silly things you wouldn't usually do. You know how it is at pajama parties, the later it gets the more things you find yourself telling the girls that you wish the next morning you hadn't revealed."

"I still think you're pretty old-fashioned, but I'll do what you say."

"I really appreciate that, Jan. Someday you will see the reason, but in the meantime, I'm glad I can count on you."

"Mother, how will I know what to order or what he can spend?"

"He should suggest several things on the menu he can afford and you could select one of them. If he says he wants either a coke or a hamburger, that's your cue. You follow suit on just a drink or a sandwich. If he says nothing, it would be better just to order a drink. If he can spend more, he might insist that you order a hamburger, too."

The big day finally arrived. Jan was dressed by five o'clock, although Tim was not due to arrive until six. She was all on edge with excitement. Her brother and sister thought she looked beautiful, and kept finding excuses to go into her room.

"Oh, Rick, I've told you a hundred times to *stay out* of here."

"I'm just trying to help you, Jan. You don't have to yell like that."

"I don't *need* any help," Jan snapped.

"Boy, you need help about yelling. If Tim could hear you now!"

"Shut up, and for the last time *get out and stay out.*"

A few minutes later, another blond head appeared at the door. "Jan, Mother says it's way early. How come you're dressed already?"

"Now look, I just told Rick to get out. You get out too, and mind your own business."

"But Jan, I just wanted to tell you how pretty you looked."

"Thanks," said Jan curtly. "Now, out!" she added not too sweetly. With an uncomprehending sigh, Lyn turned from the door.

"All this fuss just over an old date," thought Jan trying to suppress the excitement of this being her first formal one. Did she look all right? Would Tim like her dress? Dad said it was just the color of her eyes. Would he notice the little pimples that just popped out on her forehead last night? She tried to cover them the best she could, but when she looked in the mirror, they looked like headlights to her. What if she couldn't think of a thing to say, or she stumbled over his feet trying to get into the car or past him at the banquet. An hour was an awful long time to wait and her heart began to sink as she thought of one thing after another that might go wrong.

"Lyn," Jan yelled out the door. "Please tell Mother to come here." If only she could talk to Lucy, but

Mother was next best and maybe she could say something to make her feel better.

"Mother's fixing supper and she can't come right away," Lyn announced. "She'll be up after awhile. She says you have another hour yet."

"But I need her *now*. I know I have an hour."

To Jan it seemed an eternity before her mother finally came. Her smiling eyes and approving glance were reassuring.

"Oh, Mother, can you see the awful spots on my forehead?" Jan asked anxiously.

"No, the cover-up you have used keeps them from showing."

"But can't you see the bumps?"

"Maybe I could with a searchlight," her mother said with a laugh, "but they're hardly noticeable in ordinary light."

"Do I *really* look all right?"

"You look perfectly lovely, honey."

"But Mother, I'm afraid we'll run out of things to talk about."

"Honey, just be yourself. Tim asked you because he likes the way you are. Be yourself and forget that this is a formal affair and talk to him just as you do at the church steps. You always seem to have plenty to say then!"

"Yes, but that's different."

"Not really. Forget about yourself and how *you* look and feel, and think about *him*. There are lots of things you don't know about him, his interests, his travels, what his family likes to do for the summer, and what is the nicest thing that ever happened to him.

That will give you plenty to talk about. Then you can share some of your interests with him. I'm really anxious to meet this Tim. Don't forget to give me a few minutes with him after I meet him at the door. We don't want him to think you are too eager for this date!"

"I will, I will," Jan assured her mother. "But Mother, tell the kids to stay upstairs when the bell rings."

The doorbell rang fifteen minutes early. "Take your time Jan," Mrs. Sherwood called. "I'll get it."

"Mrs. Sherwood?" asked the nice-looking boy at the door.

"Yes. Do come in," Mrs. Sherwood invited cordially. "Sit down a minute. Jan will be right down. I understand your family has come here just recently."

Tim sat uneasily on the edge of the chair, but as Mrs. Sherwood talked to him, she could see him begin to relax. There was a clear look in his eyes and even though he was ill at ease, he was well-mannered. By the time Jan came into the room, the two were chatting in a friendly way.

"Mother, I want you to meet Tim Bradley. Tim, this is my mother," Jan introduced the two, feeling very uncomfortable.

"We've been having a nice visit, Jan. I know you both are going to have a wonderful time."

"What time do you want Jan home, Mrs. Sherwood?" Tim asked.

"Thank you for asking. I think about an hour or an hour and a half after the concert is over. If you are delayed, I'd appreciate your calling."

"It might be quite late, Mrs. Sherwood."

"That's all right Tim, we'll be waiting for Jan. I'm old-fashioned that way. I don't really rest until all my children are in. But don't worry about the time. I know you will try to get back and do have fun. I'll be anxious to hear all about the banquet and concert — just wish I could come, too!"

"Come on," Tim invited with a laugh.

As Jan and Tim went down the walk, an upstairs window opened and two blond heads popped out.

"Is that your boy friend, Jan?" yelled Rick in a raucous voice.

"And don't forget to say thank you," reminded Lyn cheerfully.

Jan was covered with embarrassment, but disdained to answer. Tim laughed and opened the car door for her.

What fun it was to grow up, thought Mrs. Sherwood as she closed the door behind them. This was the beginning of many interesting and yet trying days to come. If all the boys were as nice as Tim appeared to be, she wouldn't worry. There would probably be many, all different types and personalities, each contributing to help Jan find the right one, in the days to come . . . . "The right one," she thought. "How many miss the way." She must keep praying for Jan. She must teach her how to know what a boy is really like when he is not on his best behavior and trying to impress a girl.

Mrs. Sherwood waited in the darkened bedroom for Jan's return. Her husband had long since fallen asleep. "Why don't you go to sleep and let her wake you," he had suggested. But somehow she couldn't . . . .

It was with relief that she heard the car come into the driveway. In the stillness of the night their young voices could be heard.

"Thanks so much, Tim. I had a wonderful time. If it weren't so late I'd invite you in, but everything was such fun."

"I enjoyed it too, Jan. I have to be getting home anyway. See you at church."

Jan came in glowing. Mrs. Sherwood slipped quietly out of bed so as not to disturb her husband. She knew *this* was the time Jan would want to talk and to share her excitement.

"What did you think of him, Mother?"

"He seemed very nice. Was he as nice during the evening?"

"Yes, he was. It was hard to get started talking, but after we got started he was real easy to talk to and I forgot myself and had a wonderful time."

Jan described the banquet, the concert that followed, and the place they went to for cokes afterward. Mrs. Sherwood was glad she had suggested a place to Jan as Tim and Paul had no particular place in mind. Suddenly Jan collapsed — the excitement was over. She had shared everything with her mother. She was ready for bed.

"Good night, darling. I'm proud of the way you looked and acted and everything. Was it too hard coming home on time?"

"Well, yes and no. Paul and Sharon wanted to drive around after we had eaten. I hated to be a wet blanket, but I told them I had to be home, and Tim said he had promised he'd see that I was in on time too. Oh, Mother, Tim is really so nice. I'm glad now that I didn't go out with Don."

"Weren't you glad before?"

"Yes, I was, but you know how it is, Mother. I was afraid no one would ever ask me again."

Mrs. Sherwood gave Jan a good-night kiss and said nothing more. She remembered how she too felt that the world would fall apart when she had to turn down the first fellow who asked her for a date.

15

Handling Your Emotions

It was a drizzling spring day when the girls met at the bus stop as usual.

"Say, Jan, I got a letter from the camp where we were last winter. They have asked me if I would be a counselor for the summer. Wouldn't that be fun?"

"You did? So did I. Yeah, I think that would be great. Do you think your folks would let you go?"

"You know my mother doesn't care what I do. I can go if I want to!" Karin answered.

"My mother would, but I think she'd let me go. It's sure fun being a camper, but this year I think I'd like being a counselor."

"Did you get a letter, Anne?" Jan asked. "It would

be so much more fun if the three of us could go to-gether."

"Say, I wonder if some of the counselors will be guys! Maybe the lifeguard. Wouldn't we have a ball!"

The girls chattered endlessly. Rainy weather couldn't dampen the spirit of these girls as they thought of all they could do during the summer.

"Did you notice the letter said we should be at camp a week before it opened? Besides receiving special instructions for counselors, we're to help get the camp ready."

"I'll need a week to get back my wind for swim-ming," Karin remarked. "You know I didn't take swim-ming this year. I'd be winded after ten feet!"

"You're not teaching swimming, so what are you worried about?" Jan asked.

"You don't think I want any of my kids drowning do you? The lifeguard won't be able to keep an eye on *everyone*."

Excitement ran high as the girls discussed what they would take to camp, what camping would be like for two months, and whether they could stand the little kids for that length of time!

Exams . . . Shopping . . . Packing . . . Camp!

A breeze carried the pungent odor of pine through the cabin window, awakening Anne. The cot creaked as she rolled over.

"Oh, Karin look at the light creeping through the pine needles . . . . Ohhh, can you believe we're here, and here for *all* summer too?"

"What a gorgeous day!"

"I'm starved!"

"Race ya' to the dining hall. Got a lot to do today."

A counselor's days were far different from those of the carefree camper. Cabins had to be scrubbed, mattresses covered, all last season's dishes washed and the kitchen cupboards cleaned. The girls had no idea of all the work it took to get the camp into shape. Swim break was a welcome change, but after supper the crew was ready to fall into their cots for a hard-earned rest.

Mrs. Ruston, the Camp director, seemed to appreciate all that the girls were doing, but it was hard for some of them not to complain about the work.

"Home was never like this," Linda complained. "I never had to work so hard. I don't even have to make my bed at home. Imagine having to get all these beds ready. The kids ought to have to do it for themselves."

"I've helped Mother clean house, but I never had to sweep down walls and wash windows — but it's sort of fun doing it all together," Anne remarked. "Think of the mess if all the little kids tried to wash the windows! Can't you imagine how smeared they'd be?"

"That is just an old camp, I don't see why we have to get the windows so clean," Linda grumbled. "I think Mrs. Ruston is too fussy. After all, it *is* a camp. A little dirt and a few cobwebs make it more rustic," she added with a laugh.

"You're just plain lazy, Linda. Why should we be any messier at camp than at home?" Janna commented.

"We're not even this fussy at home," Linda continued. "We only clean up when there is company coming, but even then we don't bother with the places that don't show."

"Not my mother," Christine exclaimed. "We have to keep as clean and as neat as we can, but when company is coming we give the house an extra polish. I think it is only right to have the camp looking as nice as possible."

"There is one thing that really makes my mother mad," Julie added.

"What's that?" they all asked.

"Every little while she gets on the warpath and we have to give the house a real good cleaning and pick up all the junk that has gathered on the counter or the buffet. Then one of the kids will ask, 'Mother, who's coming?' 'No one's coming' she'll say, 'We're just cleaning up for our own self-respect. I want you kids to be in the habit of keeping a nice house whether anyone is coming or not.'"

"If your mother is in the habit of keeping a nice house, how come it gets messy?" one of the girls asked.

"You know how it is. Mother gets busy. We have little kids and things begin to accumulate. Mother says if she can build good habits into us now, when we are all older the house will stay tidy. It's hard for her to keep after us 'cause she is busy and active in the church, but I have to give her credit for trying! At least I know how Mrs. Ruston feels about wanting the camp to look nice when the kids come in, and then keeping it that way."

"Say, did you kids hear that we are going to have

some special talks on counseling and handling our emotions?" Dee broke in. Mrs. Ruston is having some woman from another camp come in and talk to us."

"That could be real boring, but at least it's better than cleaning." Linda commented without enthusiasm.

"It really sounds interesting to me," Christine said. "Anyway, if you don't like to clean and don't like the lectures, why did you come to Camp, Linda?"

"To be honest with you I thought it would be lots of fun with swimming, archery, and sports. I like little kids, too, but I never figured on all this work."

Pine Cone Lodge was buzzing with girls' voices, as they gathered in clusters the evening of the special talks. They sat informally around Mrs. Ruston, as she introduced Miss Patterson. Miss Patterson worked in a camp farther north training counselors for exclusive summer camps. She had spent many years observing the needs and problems of the young girls she taught.

"A camp counselor must be trained in many skills, as well as in safety regulations and ordinary habits of good health and hygiene," Miss Patterson began. You have already had instruction in these areas. Your work will also involve dealing with, and teaching youngsters how to handle their own emotions and problems. In order to be a good counselor, you have to know and understand yourself and be able to handle your own emotions sensibly.

"Of course this is easier said than done. It will help you to understand yourself as well as the children in your care if you know that there are definite reaction patterns that characterize people. There are various combinations of these reaction patterns and sometimes a person reacts in a different way under different circumstances. I will describe the main ones for you.

"All of you know the happy-go-lucky type of person — the extrovert, as they are called." The eyes of the girls turned to Jan, and several of the others. "These girls have lots of friends and are usually enthusiastic about everything they do. But often girls like this take on more than they are able to handle. They forget easily, as each new interest displaces the last. Life is so full and fascinating for them, they tend to flit from interest to interest. It will be your job as counselor to see that this type of youngster sticks to what she is doing, and finishes what she begins. She needs the camp discipline of seeing through what she begins, whether it is working for a swimming award or finishing her handcraft, before beginning something else. This girl finds it easy to quit when the going gets a little hard.

"If she wants to give up or quit or finds herself bored after a few tries, you can help her see that she needs the discipline for character building. This she should make a matter of prayer. She needs to train herself to do what she *ought* to do, not just what she *feels* like doing at the moment. They are fun to have in your cabins, but you'll probably have to keep after them about keeping the cabins tidy. They will have more ideas than you can count, but you'll need to help them sift out the practical ones, especially when it comes to stunt night, or other creative activities."

"You don't want to squelch this type of camper, but neither can you go along with *all* their ideas."

"Have you girls any questions before we go on to the next type?" Miss Patterson asked.

The girls had been listening intently from the beginning. Jan's hand went up.

"Miss Patterson, suppose the counselor finds the thing boring too. Then what do you do? There are a lot of things I begin I get sick of doing. I know how the kid feels. Do we *have to* make them do what they don't want to do? I thought camp was for fun." Some of the girls were nodding their agreement.

"Camp *is* for fun, but it is for training too. We need to teach young people that is is far more satisfying to be in control of their emotions and desires than to be controlled and at their mercy. Encourage them not to grasp at the first thing that comes along, but be selective. Help them to choose the thing they would enjoy most. Help them to see that thing through before beginning the next activity, even if they don't feel like it.

"In the Bible we are commanded that whatever our hand finds to do, to do it with all our might.[1] We ask God to take over our lives so that He can control us from within. It is really a matter of *doing* what is *right*, not just what is the easiest. There is much to be done for Christ and comparatively few who have the stick-to-itiveness to do an effective work."

"I never thought of it that way," said Jan with awe in her voice. "Guess I'll have to do a lot of disciplining of myself if I'm to set the example for the kids. It won't be easy!"

"The second type of person I want to mention is the quiet type. Often they are called introverts, but

[1] Ecclesiastes 9:10

not all quiet people are introverted. There are a lot of people who are happy, but just not bubbly like the first type I mentioned. These people do not find it so hard to finish what they begin. In fact, they take pride in doing a few things, and what they do, they do well. It is hard for them to understand the first type. Often they get very out of patience with them, feel critical and sometimes even resentful of them.

"It is hard for the quiet person to make friends, but when she makes a friend it is usually for life. Often with the outgoing person, her friends are 'out of sight out of mind!' Of course," she said, looking at Jan's cheerful expression, "this isn't always true. This is just a broad statement. As I said before these reactions are often mixed. What I mean is, a happy-go-lucky person can be a loyal friend; a serious-minded person is not necessarily critical.

"The shy and retiring girl needs to be drawn out and encouraged to try new activities. She needs to be helped to make new friends. You counselors can show the girls how to ask the others about themselves, their homes and their interests and their other friends. 'I don't know what to say to that girl,' they'll tell you, so you'll just have to start them off by telling them what to say and how to ask questions to show an interest in the other girl."

One of the girls spoke up in spite of herself. "But Miss Patterson, I'm quiet, how can I ever get my kids to make friends? I have enough trouble myself and wouldn't even have come if it hadn't been for Jan insisting. I'm terrified," Gina interjected fearfully.

"Don't worry," Miss Patterson told her sympathetically. "Some of our quiet counselors turn out to be among our best ones because they have to work at it so hard. I know it isn't easy for you, but it is no easier for the counselors who find it hard to see a thing through to stick at it. You quiet ones," she said turning to the rest, "need to turn yourselves over to God too and have Him live His life and His love out through you.

"Some quiet people tend to be self-centered, but here is where you can trust God to help you enter into the life of your youngsters. You will help to build in them the unselfishness of Christian character that is so lacking today. It isn't easy, but this is why it is so important to have your own time with God, daily. As you give yourself afresh to Him each day He'll help you to give yourself unstintingly to the kids. When you get stuck with some problem or some difficult child, ask God then and there to give you the wisdom you need and He will! Remember, He wants the kids helped and He is only waiting for you to ask Him so He can help you too.

"The third type of reaction is found in the people who see what needs to be done and can hardly wait to do it!"

"Who's that?" muttered some of the girls under their breath.

"In every organization you have these people. They are the promoters, the executives, the leaders. What they do, they do with all their heart, like the Apostle Paul. Before he was converted, he was all out for getting rid of the Christians, but after he was converted, he went all out to win people to Christ. Every organization needs people like this to get started and then to keep it going. However, these folks are tireless workers and find it hard to be sympathetic with those who cannot keep up their pace. You will find that this type, among the campers, are always on the go and looking for things to do. They work quickly and are good at a lot of things. You counselors just have to be one jump ahead of them! They need to be kept constructively occupied and challenged.

"The fourth type are the easy-going people. They are the ones who pour oil on the troubled waters. They are the peacemakers, friendly and agreeable. Among your campers, they can be teamed up with the more difficult ones. But watch that they don't get the other kids to do all their work for them! They love to do the directing, but they don't always enjoy the work. These children need to be stirred up and encouraged to enter the swimming contests and to take part in various activities. They'd just as soon sit on the side lines and watch, or hide in a corner and read a book.

"You may wonder why people react so differently and why you act as you do. This talk may help you to understand. Of course, the home that a young person comes from makes a lot of difference too. If kids have been taught to obey at home, they will obey at camp, but if they haven't, it will be harder for you to see that they obey the camp rules. However, kids know instinctively they should obey, and they respect the counselor who makes them. Some will try to get away with all they can. That's just human nature.

"When you work with the fourteen- and fifteen-year-olds, keep in mind the growing-up problems that girls that age have. You know how mixed up some of you girls felt. A lot of this mixed-up feeling came from the changes in your body. Some days you wanted to hide. Other days you loved everybody and everything, and then there were days your nerves were all on edge and you could have just screamed.

"The campers will have these up and down feelings too. Encourage them to forget themselves and just hop into the activities. Then their feelings will take care of themselves. Let them know you understand how they feel, for it was only a year or two ago that you felt the same way. God asks us to give Him our bodies, and it is at times like these that we need to turn ourselves over to Him and look to Him for one of His miracles — lifting our spirits and enabling us to act like human beings.

"Perhaps these thoughts have brought more questions to your mind. If so I'd be happy to try to answer them."

"Miss Patterson, I don't like to work, but I do like to see the work done. What's the use of looking at it? It doesn't go away and I like to get at it, and as my mother says 'get it behind me' and then do something more interesting. But my problem is that I get so mad at other kids when they go off and leave the work for me or just slop through it. I'm afraid I'll lose my temper at the kids and I would hate to do that."

"This is a good point. It won't be so hard for you when you realize that most kids enjoy a challenge. Challenge them to have the neatest cabin or to be the table who has the best manners. Just remember *you* are in charge and expect them to do what you tell them. Again, this is an area you will need wisdom from God not to be overbearing, but firm. Ask Him to give you good judgment and patience. Remember, tempers flare when an irresistible force meets an immovable object; in other words, *I* get mad when *my* will is crossed, when *I* don't get *my* way, whether it is good or bad. If the issue isn't on getting your way, but finding the *right* way, there's nothing to be angry about."

"But Miss Patterson," interjected Gina timidly, "I'd hate to be mean and spoil the kids' fun by always criticizing their work. I know that mostly they want to do it right, so that I will be pleased. I *hate* for anyone to criticize me. It makes me feel awful, and like such a flop."

"I know . . . ," said Miss Patterson gently.

"Oh," popped up Janna, oblivious to the fact that she had interrupted Miss Patterson, "I used to get all upset and cry even, when anyone criticized me, or if I didn't get an A on my work, after I'd really tried hard. But my dad would always laugh and say, 'If at first you don't succeed . . . . you'd better go back and read the instructions!' He showed me that the reason I was so upset was because I was trying to do my best, otherwise I wouldn't care. If someone criticizes your work, the thing to do is to see if what they say is true, and try to learn a better way. So now I try to remember, whenever I have to criticize the kids, to do it in a nice way. I say, I know they want to do the best they can, so they can be proud of their work, and then I tell them how to do it better. But when people forget to be nice, and say things that sound mean about me or my work, I just pretend they said it nicely, and try to find out for myself how to do better. It has really helped me."

Christine had been sitting quietly, but now, looking puzzled, she asked seriously, "Miss Patterson, I was in a cabin last year with one girl who would get terribly moody. She would just want to stay in her bunk and be left alone. One day I stayed too, and she got to talking to me. It was awful — the things she was thinking. She said horrible things about our counselor, and she said she just hated one of the other girls, and kept thinking all kinds of mean things about her all the time. It's no wonder she was unfriendly and quiet so much of the time, thinking such awful things! What would I ever do if I had a camper like that in my cabin?"

"All of us have times when we are moody, or when our feelings have been hurt. Then unkind thoughts enter our minds. If we dwell on them and indulge our feelings, we can easily acquire the habit of self-pity. You'd have to take this girl aside and talk to her very gently, lovingly, and firmly about her thought life. Tell her that we can sin just as much by what we *think* as by what we *do*, and more than that, the things we *do* will always be colored by the things we *think*. That's why God tells us in His Word that as a man 'thinketh in his heart, so is he,'[2] and 'Keep thy heart with all diligence; for out of it are the issues of life.'[3] After you have shown her the importance of keeping her thoughts pure toward others, you can help her learn to turn to God for His help, whenever these thoughts arise, and to then just refuse to think about them. God will help her, but she must deliberately turn to something that is pleasant and interesting to do, even if she doesn't feel like it. Soon her mind

[2] Proverbs 23:7
[3] Proverbs 4:23

will be taken up with the new thing and the feelings will disappear because she hasn't fed them. In this way she can keep her mind free of evil thoughts. She may need your help until she has built the habit of resisting the evil and turning to the good.

"Counseling is such a satisfying experience. I know you girls will love it. Just think of your wonderful responsibility. You are here to help train and develop girls in every area of their lives. Girls need to see that right reactions will make them more able to face their daily problems. You can share with them the helpful experiences that you have had.

"The purpose of a Christian Camp is to build up girls mentally, physically, emotionally, and spiritually and to teach them to delight in doing the will of God."

Back in the counselors cabin Anne expressed the girls' thoughts.

"Miss Patterson sure makes it sound like an important job. I just thought about all the fun we'd have, but there's sure a lot more to being a counselor than fun."

"Yeah, there sure is — according to her . . . ."

"It's sort of like 'making grownups' isn't it?"

"I never thought of it like that before, but that's what has been happening to us all along!"

Jan's face suddenly brightened. "That's what Miss Marshall was trying to say. *What you are today will determine what you will be tomorrow!*"